MURDER
& CRIME

ESSEX

MURDER
& CRIME

ESSEX

MARTYN LOCKWOOD

The
History
Press

First published 2011

The History Press
The Mill, Brimscombe Port
Stroud, Gloucestershire, GL5 2QG
www.thehistorypress.co.uk

British Library Cataloguing in Publication Data.
A catalogue record for this book is available from the British Library.

ISBN 978 0 7524 6083 3

Typesetting and origination by The History Press
Printed in Great Britain

CONTENTS

ACKNOWLEDGEMENTS

The author would like to thank the Chief Constable, the Essex Police Authority and the Trustees of the Essex Police Museum for the use of photographs and other material from their collection.

A number of people have contributed in the preparation of this book and I am particularly indebted to Peter Durr for allowing the use of his article on the Little Leighs Body Snatchers (see chapter 8); and to Andy Begent for the use of his article on executions at Springfield Prison (see chapter 15). I have used material from a number of History Notebooks which have been produced by the Essex Police Museum by a number of different authors, although in each case I have checked the facts against original material and by referring to the reports of the court proceedings, which were extensively reported in local newspapers including the *Chelmsford Chronicle*, *Essex Standard*, and also several national newspapers.

I believe I have obtained permission to use the photographs where necessary, or they are now out of copyright. If I have breached any copyright, my apologies.

The Essex Police Museum was founded in 1991. It is a registered charity and is open to members of the public to visit. Details of opening times and services which the museum offers can be found by visiting the website: www.essex.police.uk/museum

INTRODUCTION

Murder & Crime in Essex brings together a number murderous tales, and other crimes, which have taken place in Essex over the past 200 years. Some of the stories included in this book will be little known outside Essex, while others made national headlines at the time they were committed. It was a conscious decision not to include any case later than 1950 and to cover cases that occurred in the area covered by the Essex County Constabulary, thus excluding cases that occurred in Metropolitan Essex and policed by the Metropolitan Police.

A number of books have been written on crime in Essex and so I have included cases that have not previously been given wide coverage, and excluded those which have appeared time and time again and about which there is little new to say. I have also included some background information to enable the reader to better understand the subject matter.

Martyn Lockwood, 2011

One

THE MURDER OF HENRY TRIGG

Berden is a small village which lies some five miles north of Bishop Stortford. In 1814 there were around 300 souls living in the village, the majority of whom earned their living from the land. There were also a few tradesmen, including Henry Trigg, the village shoemaker. Trigg was 36 years old and lived with his parents at his shop, which was situated in The Street next to Berden Hall. He was in the habit of sleeping on the ground floor of the shop while his elderly parents slept on the floor above. Trigg was also the Parish Constable for Berden.

Before the Rural Constabulary Act of 1839 and the establishment of the Essex County Constabulary, there was no police force in the modern sense of the word; maintaining law and order was a local matter. Unlike some other offices, that of constable did not have a property qualification and every householder in the parish was liable to serve. The role of parish constable evolved from the old manorial position of 'head borough' or 'tithingman' and grew steadily into much more than a mere preserver of local peace. Duties varied by time and place, but among the long list of those that a constable had to undertake were: apprehending vagrants and offenders; keeping offenders in custody until the sessions; serving writs and summonses; maintaining lists of jurors; inspecting public houses; checking weights and measures; supporting bailiffs at evictions; and collecting duties and taxes.

The post of parish constable was an established one, and although its origins are unclear, it is thought by some to date back as far as King Alfred's time.

The *Chelmsford Chronicle*, in its edition of Friday, 1 April 1814, reported, 'A most atrocious murder was committed on the night of Friday last at Berden'.

On the night of 25 March, two men from Bishop Stortford came to the village. One man, Thomas Turner, had made a previous visit to buy a dog from a man named Chapman and had noticed an abundance of leather in Trigg's shop. He told his friend, William Pratt, and the two men decided to relieve the shop of its stock. Pratt was described as 'a well looking man, with fair hair and good complexion, about 5 feet 10 inches in height'. Turner was described as 'considerably shorter, a squat figure with a rather disagreeable obliquity of vision in his left eye'. They carried a dark lanthorn (a lantern whose light could be covered) with them. Pratt was also armed with a pistol.

Shortly before midnight, Henry Trigg was woken by a noise and went to his parents' room and said that he believed there were intruders in the shop. His father then followed him down to the shop, where they found the two men. Henry Trigg immediately set about Turner with his staff, causing him to fall to the floor where Trigg continued to beat him, his father exhorting him to 'dress him well'. Trigg senior was then attacked by Pratt, who fired the gun he was holding. The shot fortunately missed the old man, but it had the effect of causing the Triggs to draw back. As Turner was getting to his feet Pratt fired a second shot, shouting, 'Now damn your heart, I will do for you.' The bullet passed directly through the young man's heart and he collapsed dead on the floor.

The two men ran from the shop and the village was roused by the cries of the elderly couple. Left at the scene of the crime were a hat and the dark lanthorn. Despite a search of the area, no trace of the men was discovered and even the exertions of two Bow Street Runners, Messrs Vickery and Bishop, who were called in to investigate the outrage, failed to make any headway and find those responsible for the murder. A year was to pass before the *Chelmsford Chronicle* reported on 17 February 1815 the arrest of Turner and Pratt by the Runners in Bishop Stortford. They had been arrested after 'a whisper' regarding a series of robberies in Hertfordshire. The two men were also charged with the murder of Henry Trigg and were committed for trial at the Lent Assize at Chelmsford.

The Shire Hall, Chelmsford, where the Essex Assizes were held and where Chapman and Pratt were tried for the murder of Henry Trigg.

Moulsham Gaol, Chelmsford. Built in 1782, it remained in use until 1826, when a new gaol was built at Springfield. Chapman and Pratt were executed on a spot just outside the gaol before a large crowd of onlookers.

The *Chelmsford Chronicle* on 17 March reported details of the trial of the two men. Witnesses called by the prosecution included Mr and Mrs Trigg. Henry's mother told the court that her son had 'dropped like a bird' when shot. Stafford, the Bow Street Runner in Chief, gave evidence of the arrest of the two men. He told the court that a search of their homes revealed picklocks, pistols and a dark lanthorn. He also said that he clapped the hat found at the scene of the murder on Turner's head and it was found to 'fit most snugly'. Turner, of course, claimed that this was hardly evidence to implicate him in the crime.

The two men were held in separate cells in the gaol at Hertford, 'removed from the dreadful course of life which they had been accustomed to pursue, the remorse of their consciences compelled a full disclosure of their crimes.' Neither man at the trial denied making their confessions and the prosecutor expressed a hope that 'their fate would not be thrown away upon the common people of the county – poaching leads to stealing, stealing to housebreaking and housebreaking to murder.'

The two men blamed each other for the crime, but to no avail. The law at that time was clear – that when persons were collectively involved in an illegal enterprise, they were responsible for its results. The jury had no hesitation in convicting Pratt and Turner of the murder.

Mr Justice Chambre then pronounced the sentence of the law upon the prisoners, whom, it was noted, seemed very little affected by their situation.

By the time the readers of the *Chronicle* had digested this information the prisoners had been dead for four days. Along with two other convicted murderers, William Seymour and Thomas Scandling, who had been sentenced to death at the same Assize, they were taken to a spot outside Moulsham Gaol. It was reported that, 'a greater number of persons were spectators of this

The neglected grave of Henry Trigg lies in a quiet corner in Berden churchyard.

scene than has been observed for a length of time'. All prisoners acknowledged their guilt, but neither Pratt nor Turner implicated any accomplice, though it was thought at the time that others were involved in some of the other crimes they had committed. All four men were then hanged.

The *Chelmsford Chronicle* extract ends: 'The bodies of Pratt and Turner were carried away by some professional gentlemen who reside in the neighbourhood where the murder was committed.'

In the western part of the churchyard of St Nicholas's churchyard at Berden is the grave of Henry Trigg. The inscription on the headstone reads:

In memory of Henry Trigg of this parish aged 36 years, who was murdered March 25th 1814 endeavouring to protect his property, March 13th 1815 Wm Pratt, Thos Turner both of Bishops Stortford, Herts, were executed at Chelmsford for the above offence on their own confession.

TWO

POACHING

Stories of poaching and poachers sometimes conjure up a romantic image of poor villagers taking a rabbit to feed their starving families. Indeed, it was seen by the majority of the poor simply as a defence of tradition. Since time immemorial local people had, by tradition, hunted rabbits and other game on 'Common' land. The poacher in many areas was seen as something of a popular hero. Whilst this image in part was true, the reality was often more sinister. In the early nineteenth century, it was claimed that one out of every four inmates in England's prisons was an offender against the game laws and poaching was widely regarded as one of the fastest growing crimes in the country.

By no means all poaching involved poor people defending their traditional way of life. Gangs of professional poachers hunted game and then sold it on the black market to local innkeepers, who would often turn a blind eye. Men could make a good living from poaching.

From the time of Richard II (1389 until 1831), no person was allowed to kill game unless qualified by estate or social standing. In the nineteenth century, legislation, including the Night Poaching Acts of 1828 and 1844, the Game Act of 1831, the Poaching Prevention Act 1862, and the Ground Game Acts of 1880 and 1906, were enacted to prevent people taking game unlawfully and harsh punishments were meted out to those who were caught. The game laws of 1830 had a graded scale for poaching. For the first offence the punishment was three months' hard labour, six months for the second offence and the possibility of seven years' transportation or two years' hard labour for the third. Hostility to the game laws was however aggravated in 1862 by the passing of the Poaching Prevention Act, which allowed the police to search any person on the road, or in a public place, whom they suspected of poaching, or having in their possession a gun, nets, or snares for the purpose of killing or taking game.

Men became desperate and violence was often offered to gamekeepers and police officers if they were surprised carrying out their night-time activities – sometimes with

'The English Gamekeeper'. Etching by Richard Ansdell, RA (1815-1885).

fatal results. Between November 1880 and July 1896, there were at least thirty serious affrays involving poachers and gamekeepers in various parts of the country. In seventeen of these cases, either poachers or keepers were killed.

In March 1829 the *Chelmsford Chronicle* reported the trial of a gang of men, fifteen in number, for 'maliciously and feloniously shooting at Richard Warren with powder, and intent to kill and murder.' After a trial lasting several days, seven of the accused were sentenced to transportation for fourteen years, seven to transportation for seven years and one man received a sentence of twelve months' imprisonment with hard labour.

It appears that poaching in the Stansted area was prevalent at the time. The Newport Magistrates had heard a case in November 1850, where six 'desperadoes' of Bishop's Stortford were charged with 'night poaching', which included a murderous attack on gamekeeper John Wilkins. It was reported that before they finally felled him, Wilkins was defending himself with a gun (which was smashed and discharged during the struggle) in one hand, and a hanger (or small sword) in the other.

In March 1856, four men, brothers James (29), Thomas (23) and William (22) Thurgood, and James Guiver (30), were brought before the Assize court at Chelmsford, charged with the wilful murder of gamekeeper William Hales at Boreham, on land in the occupation of Sir John Tyrell.

The evidence presented at the court was that the four men, all labourers, each armed with a gun, had set out for a nights' poaching in woods belonging to Sir John. The sound of shots attracted the attention of three gamekeepers, who split up to try and locate the men. One of the keepers, John Hales, was heard to shout, 'Come on mates, here they are.' Joseph Wesby, another keeper, heard a shot and saw Hales fall to the ground. Joseph and his father James managed to detain James Thurgood and take him back to Dukes Head Farm. When they returned to the wood they found the body of Hales.

The four men appeared before the Grand Jury, who withdrew the capital offence against three of the men, causing James Thurgood to face trial for murder on his own. At the trial it could not be ascertained who had fired the fatal shot but Thurgood was nevertheless found guilty of being an accessory to murder and sentenced to death. His reply on being sentenced was, 'Thank you sir; God bless you all.' The sentence was later commuted to imprisonment. Charges of night poaching were met with guilty pleas and each defendant was given four years' penal servitude.

In November 1872, Thomas Dudley, gamekeeper for Sir Thomas Western, Lord Lieutenant of Essex, was fatally shot by poachers while he patrolled the estate at Braxted. Three men were arrested, including William Bundock. He was sent for trial but the jury decided that the firearm was discharged in panic. The judge told Bundock that he was lucky not to have been convicted of a capital crime, but having been found guilty of poaching with violence, he was sentenced to five years' penal servitude. The two other men involved in the crime received four months' hard labour.

In January 1873, gamekeepers on the estate of Sir Thomas Western at Rivenhall spotted six poachers armed with guns and sticks, led by one of the estate's grooms, Alexander 'Racer' Cowell. Surprised by the gamekeepers, a vicious fight ensued between the two groups, the poachers getting the upper hand and injuries being caused to the gamekeepers, who retired from the fray. One keeper was struck on the head by a shotgun stock. Unfortunately for Cowell he had been recognised, and the next day was arrested by the police at Braintree and subsequently brought before the Spring Assizes at Chelmsford. The judge decided to 'make an example of him' and Cowell received a sentence of five years' penal servitude.

In October 1881 John Prior, a gamekeeper employed by Lord Braybrooke of Audley End, was shot and killed in an exchange with a poacher. The person responsible, William Wright, was arrested and tried at the Assizes, where he was convicted and sentenced to death, the sentence later being commuted to penal servitude for life.

Assaults on police officers were all too common. PC Walter Chandler was promoted to the Merit Class on 17 February 1883 for his courageous conduct in apprehending a notorious poacher, who was armed with a gun. Chandler heard the discharge of guns in the direction of Dengie, so he placed himself at the residence of a notorious poacher, James Bone, in the village of Tillingham. At 1.30 a.m. Chandler saw Bone arrive home with bulky pockets. He challenged the man, who ran off. PC Chandler gave chase and

The Merit Star was awarded to PC Walter Chandler for his courageous conduct in apprehending a notorious poacher armed with a gun in 1883.

a double-barrelled shotgun was leveled at the constable. A violent struggle ensued and Chandler managed to wrench the weapon from him and knock Bone down. When searched, he was found in possession of hares. James Bone was described in court as 'a most notorious, daring and clever poacher, rarely known to work and who obtained his living entirely by poaching'. Bone was fined £4 with costs of 8s 6d and in default of payment was committed to prison for one calendar month.

However, on other occasions it was the gamekeeper who faced the court. In July 1820, Edward Lodge, a gamekeeper employed by a T.F. Fane, Esq., of Doddinghurst, near Brentwood, appeared at the Essex Assizes charged with the murder of James Mingay, by shooting him with a gun loaded with powder and bullet. The deceased man was described as a 'labouring man, confessedly addicted to poaching.' The court heard that Lodge had disturbed Mingay, who was armed with a gun and poaching pheasants, had fired both barrels of his gun at him and wounded him in the groin. It was further alleged that Lodge left the dying man, who managed to crawl to a nearby house, where he told a man named Day what had happened. A surgeon was called and a Magistrate, Archdeacon Woolaston, attended and took down Mingay's dying deposition.

The prisoner in his defence submitted a written paper to the court, which read:

It is, and ever will be a matter of regret to me, that I should be the cause of the death of a fellow creature; but hearing and believing that there were other men in Dogwood, I was actuated from fear that my own life was in danger.

Witnesses were called who gave evidence that the deceased was indeed a notorious poacher and who had expressed great hostility to gamekeepers. The jury deliberated for five minutes on their verdict, finding the defendant guilty of manslaughter. Lodge was sentenced to nine months' imprisonment.

Three

THE MURDER OF
SERGEANT EVES

Adam John Eves, a native of Hutton, near Brentwood, joined the Essex County Constabulary at the age of 20 in March 1877 and was appointed constable number 63. He served at various stations throughout the county before being promoted to the rank of Acting Sergeant and posted to the village of Purleigh, near Maldon, in January 1891. By the spring of 1893 he would be dead – brutally murdered whilst carrying out his duties.

Eves had been a wheelwright before joining the police. In line with other constables who joined at this time, he entered upon a career that demanded almost unremitting hard work performed under conditions of severe hardship. Assaults on constables were common and in the course of their duty they would be expected to walk upwards of 20 miles a day. Meal breaks were uncommon, officers were expected to eat on duty; and it was not until 1910 that they were granted a weekly rest day. In exchange a constable received a weekly wage that left him, and his family if he had one, near to the breadline. On joining, Eves, as a constable 3rd class, received a salary of 21s per week – similar to that of an agricultural labourer.

Discipline was strict and punishment imposed arbitrarily. The Chief Constable was the sole disciplinary authority, with power to fine, reduce in class or rank, or dismiss any officer who appeared before him charged with a breach of discipline.

Eves, who married in 1878, lived with his wife Elizabeth in a small cottage at Purleigh, which also served as the local police station. He was a popular officer in the district, who could be relied upon to discharge his duties diligently. However, in the course of his work he had made a number of enemies amongst the criminal classes, and had been threatened on more than one occasion with violence.

On the evening of Saturday, 15 April 1893, Eves set out on his usual patrol of the district. About 10 p.m. he called in at the Royal Oak public house, where he spoke to the landlord and handed him a reward notice concerning the poisoning of rooks in the district. Due to come off duty at midnight, his wife was not unduly alarmed when he failed to return and she

went to bed. When she awoke the next morning and found he had not returned, she comforted herself with the thought that he had been detained by a fire in the district. However, as the day progressed she became more and more alarmed by his absence. At 2.30 p.m. that Sunday afternoon, Herbert Patten, a local carpenter, was walking past the Eves' cottage with his girlfriend. Mrs Eves asked Patten if he had any knowledge of a fire in the district. He told her that he had not heard of any fire, whereupon she said, 'You never know whether they're going to be brought home dead or alive.'

Puzzled by the remark, Patten and his girlfriend continued on their walk across the fields at Hazeleigh Hall Farm, which lay about a mile from Purleigh. As they approached a spot known locally as Bellrope Gate, Patten noticed that the ground had been disturbed and, looking down, he saw to his alarm that the grass was saturated with blood. Nervously, he looked into the deep ditch nearby and recoiled in horror as he saw the body of Adam Eves lying at the bottom, in six inches of water. Eves had suffered dreadful injuries, the body was terribly mutilated and his throat had been slashed from ear to ear.

Patten ran for help to Stow Manes, where the nearest constable lived. He told the astonished Constable Chaplin of his discovery and the two men hurried back to the scene of the murder. On their way they came across Inspector Pryke, who was in the area making enquiries into the theft of corn from a barn at Hazeleigh Hall Farm during the night. Together the Inspector and PC Chaplin examined the mutilated body of Sergeant Eves. They noticed that his truncheon was still in his pocket and the shutter on his bulls-eye lamp was in the 'off' position. As they moved the body they found three stout sticks lying underneath. One stick was broken into three pieces; all were soaked in blood. A search revealed both a bloodstained spade and three corn sacks lying nearby. A trail of spilled corn led towards Bell Rope Gate. The two officers also noticed a set of wheel marks in the grass leading from the scene to a group of nearby cottages.

The body of the dead officer was moved to his home. Superintendent Halsey telegraphed the Chief Constable, Captain Showers, with the news of the murder. He immediately sent two officers, Inspector Terry and Detective Sergeant Dale, to Purleigh to assist in the investigation. Setting up their headquarters at the Bell Inn, initial enquiries revealed that several threats had been made against the dead officer and only a short time before his death he told a villager that one man had said, 'If ever I get the chance at you, I'll take you.' Suspicion at an early stage fell on a group of men from the village, all petty criminals with bad reputations. In July 1891, Eves had been assaulted by one of these men, John Davis, whom he had arrested for poaching. For this assault Davis had received two months imprisonment with hard labour.

Inspector Pryke was dealing with a theft of corn which had occurred at Hazeleigh Hall Farm. It had been reported on the Sunday morning to the police by the son of the farm bailiff, Joseph Moss, who had discovered that attempts had been made to force the door on the granary. Pryke's enquiries into the theft showed that false entries had been made in the farm ledger and a greater quantity of corn had been stored in the barn than was shown. Edward Fitch, the owner of the farm estimated some 13 bushels of corn were missing. The police now had a possible motive for the murder. Had Eves come across the men as they carried the stolen corn away from the farm, tried to arrest them and for his efforts had been killed?

The Essex Constabulary acted swiftly, and on the Monday morning Inspector Terry and Sergeant Dale visited the house of John Davis, a 34-year-old labourer. Finding no one at home they then called at the home of his 30-year-old brother, Richard, also a labourer. Outside the house they noticed a handcart, and looking in it they saw stains which appeared to be blood. Both brothers were arrested. A search was made of the pond in Richard Davis' garden and police recovered three sacks of corn. This corn and that found scattered at the scene was similar to that stored in the barn.

Other arrests took place that day. Charles Sales, a 47-year-old dealer, and John Bateman, aged 37, were arrested by Superintendent Halsey and Inspector Pryke. All four were local men, well known in the locality and each had previous convictions for theft and poaching. They had worked together in the past and had recently been engaged in threshing corn at Hazeleigh Hall Farm. When Sales was arrested, bloodstains were found on his waistcoat cart, caused he said, by a bone he had bought. The blood in John Davis' cart was, he told police, from a sheep's head which he had bought in Maldon on the previous Saturday. Blood was also found on the back of Richard Davis' coat and shoes. Bateman's clothes were stained – he explained this had been caused by porter from the public house. When interviewed, Bateman admitted to the police that he had been lying out all night in a field near where Eves was murdered. All four men were remanded in custody and conveyed to Chelmsford Prison for a week.

The police officers who investigated the murder of Acting Sergeant Adam Eves. Superintendent Halsey is in the centre of the group with Inspector Pryke on his right.

On Wednesday morning, a villager named Thomas Choat went to the police and made a statement concerning a James Ramsey and his son John. Ramsey had been the driver of the threshing machine at Hazeleigh Hall Farm, his son the chaff boy, and Choat had been the feeder for the threshing machine. He told police he had heard James Ramsey make threats against Eves and on the Monday after the murder Ramsey had turned up for work wearing new clothes. Ramsey and his son were arrested and taken to Maldon police station. A search of their home revealed a pair of blood-soaked trousers and Choat told the police that James Ramsey had worn them on the Saturday. Sacks similar to those used to steal wheat were found concealed under his mattress. The two Ramsey's were remanded in custody until the following Monday.

On 24 May 1893, John and Richard Davis, Charles Sales and James Ramsey were committed for trial at the next Essex Assize. The case against John Bateman and John Ramsey was dropped due to insufficient evidence.

The trial commenced at the Assize court at Chelmsford on 3 August 1893, before Mr Justice Mathew. All four prisoners pleaded not guilty to the charge that they had murdered Sergeant Eves. Mr Crump QC opened the case for the prosecution and outlined the evidence to the hushed court. The four men, he said, had been involved in the theft of corn from Hazeleigh Hall Farm, where they worked. PC Eves, on his way home on that fateful night, had come across the men making their way from the farm with their sacks of stolen wheat. Challenged by Eves, they had set about him and murdered him, throwing his body into the ditch, where it was found by Patten. Evidence of the cart tracks was introduced. Ownership of the cart was never disputed by Richard Davis and he had told police he had used it to collect stones from the very field where the murder took place. The spade found at the scene near the body was identified as belonging to him.

On the second day of the trial, the case against Sale was dismissed and he was discharged. The defence called no witnesses. Ramsey and the Davis brothers maintained their innocence, claiming they were in bed asleep on the night of the murder. Their only defence to the charge was that other men worked at the farm and had the opportunity to steal the corn, inferring that the evidence produced by the prosecution was purely circumstantial. In his summing up, Mr Justice Mathew told the jury that the theft had been planned. The tally at the farm had been altered and those who had stolen the corn had murdered Eves. The jury retired at 3.26 p.m. and returned at 4.46 p.m. They found the two brothers 'guilty', but James Ramsey 'not guilty'. The judge donned the black cap and amid the deafening silence of the courtroom he pronounced sentence of death, telling the men not to hold out any hope of a pardon in this world, 'From the Almighty, as I hope with penitence and contrition you will obtain forgiveness for your most grievous sin.'

Richard Davis lodged an appeal against his conviction. His brother John, resigned to his fate, confessed to the murder. He said that all three men had been involved in the theft of the corn. As they struggled on the ground, Ramsey came up and struck a number of blows to Eves' head with his cudgel. His brother Richard had played no part in the assault and, as the unconscious officer lay on the ground, Ramsey cut his throat with his knife. The three of them then threw the body in the ditch. Richard Davis was later reprieved and sentenced to imprisonment for life. John Davis paid the ultimate penalty by being hanged at Chelmsford Gaol on 16 August 1893.

The story might have ended there, but James Ramsey, who had been cleared of the murder, was charged with breaking and entering the barn at Hazeleigh Hall Farm and stealing thirteen and a half bushels of corn. He was brought before Chelmsford Assizes in November 1893 to be tried before Lord Chief Justice Coleridge.

Selina, the wife of the late John Davis, who had been prevented from giving evidence at the trial of her husband, was now called as a witness for the prosecution. She told the court that at 9 p.m. on the night of the murder she was at home and was about to go to bed, when she heard a knock at the door. James Ramsey entered carrying a bundle of sacks. She left her husband talking to him but heard them leave the house about an hour later. Richard Davis was brought from prison to give evidence. He told the court that on the night in question he was asleep at his cottage when he heard a knock at the window. Looking out he saw his brother John. He got dressed and went to his brother's cottage, where he found him with James Ramsey. John Davis had two bundles of sacks and Ramsey had one. They all left the house, the two men telling Richard that they were going to Hazeleigh Hall Farm to steal some of the wheat they had been threshing. They went to the barn, and, after some difficulty forcing the door, they eventually crawled in, where they set about the task of filling their sacks. Three sacks were taken outside and hidden in a gap in the hedge while the three took a further sack each and made their way to their own homes.

The court was hushed as Davis continued. The three men were walking across the field. Richard led, followed by John with Ramsey bringing up the rear. Suddenly Richard heard his brother call out to him and heard the sound of a scuffle in the darkness. He turned to see his brother, Ramsey and Sergeant Eves rolling about on the ground. Davis was asked, 'What condition was the police sergeant in?' Davis replied, 'He was quite dead.'

The grave of Acting Sergeant Adam Eves in Purleigh churchyard.

IN MEMORIAM
SERGEANT ADAM JOHN EVES
ESSEX CONSTABULARY
WHO WAS MURDERED WHILE IN
THE EXECUTION OF HIS DUTY
15TH APRIL 1893
AGED 36 YEARS.

THIS TABLET IS ERECTED BY THE
WHOLE OF HIS BROTHER OFFICERS OF
ALL RANKS AS A MARK OF ESTEEM AND
REGARD FOR HIS BRAVERY.

He then told the court that he had taken no part in the fight and was abused later by Ramsey for not coming to their assistance. John told him later that he had struck Eves with his stick and that Ramsey had cut his throat. The three men then threw the body into the ditch where it was found by Patten. The three sacks of corn they had with them were hidden in the nearby pond. Their clothes were bloodstained and Ramsey said he would burn his when he got home.

Davis was cross-examined by Ramsey. Ramsey accused the two brothers of the murder: 'That man was not killed in a minute. You and your brother knocked him about and left him for dead. I never touched him. You went home and got a spade to bury him. When you returned he was still alive. You knocked him about till his poor head was in pieces.' Davis replied, 'You did it, and no one else. You put him in the ditch.'

In his summing up, His Lordship told the jury that from Ramsey's description of the crime he had been at the spot himself, and stood guilty on his own confession. The jury found him guilty without leaving the court. Ramsey was sentenced to fourteen years' penal servitude. In his address to the prisoner, His Lordship said, 'I should ill discharge my duty if shortened by one single hour the sentence, which may be passed on you.'

The funeral of Sergeant Eves took place at Purleigh church a week after the murder. The cortège was led by the Chief Constable and over 150 members of the Essex Constabulary attended. Eves was held in such high esteem in the neighbourhood that the route to the church was thronged with grieving villagers. His widow was awarded the maximum pension payable at that time, £15 per year. A public subscription raised the considerable sum of £400. Mrs Eves continued to live in the village.

Four

'DEAR DR PAGET, I HAVE SHOT A BURGLAR'

'On Thursday morning the 29th February 1849, the inhabitants of Great Chesterford, Saffron Walden and the neighbourhood were excited to a remarkable degree by a report that a desperate attempt at burglary had been made at a lone farmhouse, about two miles from the Chesterford station.' So the *Chelmsford Chronicle* reported in an article entitled a 'Desperate Burglary'.

The burglary had occurred at Strethall Hall, which lay in the village of Strethall, some two miles from Great Chesterford. The house was described as an old-fashioned building, placed in a lonely position upon a hill near the church, and at some distance from any other houses or cottages. Strethall is possibly one of the smallest parishes in the country, consisting only of twenty to thirty souls.

The house was owned by Nehemiah Perry, aged over 60, and described as 'an opulent and highly respectable landowner and occupier.' He lived with his brother, Thomas, and their housekeeper, Rebecca Nash.

Nehemiah had thirty years before been married to a gypsy by whom he had a family, a daughter marrying a local surgeon. However, his wife would not settle and went back to the gypsy life and they were subsequently divorced. Because of the bad blood that existed between himself and the gypsies, Nehemiah was worried they might visit him with revenge in mind and so he was in the habit of taking a loaded gun with him when he went to bed.

On the night of Wednesday, 28 February 1849, the brothers retired to their beds as usual, a little after 10 p.m. At one o'clock in the morning, Nehemiah was woken by a noise down stairs and from the sound he thought the back door had been broken open. Jumping out of bed he heard the sound of a second door being broken open. Arming himself with the gun he kept by the side of his bed, he called out to Thomas, 'Hall-ope Master Thomas, there's something up.' The brothers went to the top of the stairs where they saw the figure of a man with a light in his left hand, and carrying a pistol in his right, climbing the stairs.

The man's face was covered and he was wearing a hat. Behind him Nehemiah saw a second figure on the stairs.

Believing that this constituted a threat to his life, Nehemiah did not hesitate, but fired his gun and the first man fell. Nehemiah said to Thomas, 'Don't be frightened, there's one; all right I've snuffed his candle for him.' The sound of the gun going off woke the housekeeper, but Thomas told her to stay in her room. They heard the sound of the fallen burglar dragged off but did not hear anyone leave the house. The brothers, fearing there were a number of men still in the house, remained on guard at the top of the stairs until about five o'clock, when they made their way carefully downstairs where, in a back room, they found the body of a man, who had been shot through the breastbone. His waistcoat was unbuttoned and his shirt drawn up as if someone had looked to see where he had been shot. He was wearing shoes with stockings over the top. A sacking mask lay near the body and under a broken window in the parlour lay a bludgeon.

Police Constable William Miller, the village policeman at nearby Elmdon, was called and began his investigation. Noting the broken window, he examined the outside of the house and saw the footprints of four persons in the snow. Miller sent a message to Superintendent Clarke at Littlebury who arrived at the hall at nine o'clock. He searched the body of the dead man, and apart from a small amount of money he only had a pipe, a pair of pliers and a knife in his possession. However, there was nothing on the body to identify him, although Clarke thought he had spotted the man some days before on the road between Chesterford and Newport. A description of the man was circulated to all surrounding police forces in the hope that someone would recognise the man.

As a result a Miss Tofts, who lived in a remote farmhouse near Cambridge, had no doubt it was the same ruffian – one of a gang of four or five burglars – who she had seen in her bedroom earlier in the month. Interestingly in this case, the gang may have been captured had two policeman acted more responsibly. Mr Tofts, hearing the commotion in the house, jumped out of the window and ran in his nightgown into town, where he was arrested by the two policemen who though he was insane. It was only at the police station that wiser counsel prevailed, but by this time the gang had escaped.

News of the shooting travelled fast and soon the whole village came to view the body. Crime scene investigations were still a thing of the future, and people from far and wide were allowed to trample round the corpse, which Superintendent Clarke had sat up against a wall, at one point wearing his hat.

An inquest was opened before Mr C. Lewis, the coroner, consisting of 'agriculturalists' and which was convened at Perry's home to look into the facts surrounding the death of the unknown man and a number of witnesses were called to give evidence. The coroner addressed the jury, saying that the facts were so exceedingly clear, plain and simple, that many remarks from him were unnecessary; for if they were satisfied that Mr Perry's life and property were in peril after the house had been broken into, as evidently it was, it was his duty to tell them that their verdict would be justifiable homicide, for it was clear that when a man's life and property were in danger he was perfectly justified in shooting any man so endangering them. The jury unanimously agreed with the coroner.

The next problem was one of hygiene, as the body had still not been identified. The coroner gave Superintendent Clarke his permission to leave the body unburied, in the

St Mary the Virgin, Strethall, where the body of 'Little Abel' was placed in the belfry in an effort to identify him.

hope that someone might come forward and identify him. It was then put into a coffin and placed in the belfry of Strethall church, where the ever-practical Nehemiah charged three pence for people to view it.

The *Chelmsford Chronicle* continued:

> Various officers and others have seen the body of the dead man; indeed, hundreds of people have visited the place; but no one has been able to identify him, although some assert that he has been in the neighbourhood during the past year with a nut-stall and target. His countenance is of a very forbidding kind and his head bears a general resemblance to that of Daniel Good, who was hung for murder some time ago in London. Some silver and several false keys were found in his pocket. He appears to be about 30 years of age; 5ft 4in in height; sallow complexion, dark hair, the whiskers appear to have been worn large, but have recently been very closely trimmed and left very narrow; he appears to have been quite clean shaved within a short time of his death. His right tooth is out. He had on a white shirt, black and white neckerchief, one white cotton stocking, blucher boots tied in three holes, cord trousers, drab cloth double-breasted waistcoat, stout blue cloth coat with pockets inside, black Paris hat, apparently bought at Peterborough; a large pair of worsted stocking were drawn over his shoes, and this plan seems to have been adopted by the whole of the gang.

Finally, Benjamin Taylor, a police officer from Peterborough, made an identification, helped by marks and details from Gaol books. The corpse was in fact that of one Abraham Green, alias Woods, alias 'Little Abel', a ne'er do well known throughout East Anglia.

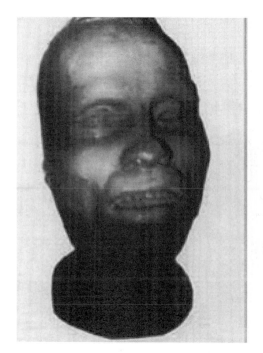

The death mask of 'Little Abel' and a line drawing indicating what he may have looked like.

Although Green had a wife, she did not claim his body and so Nemehiah packed it into a large game-basket and sent it to Dr (later Sir George) Paget, a distinguished surgeon and pathologist at Cambridge, with a cryptic note attached: 'Dear Dr Paget, I have shot a burglar. N. Perry.' Bodies for vivisection were hard to come by and no doubt it was a welcome present.

In the meantime, the police had not been inactive. Two men, William Goody, aged 21 and from Halstead, but 'well known in Chelmsford,' and William Palmer of Ashby-de-la-Zouch, a 26-year-old hawker, were detained on suspicion of being involved in the burglary of Mr Perry's house. The two men were remanded in custody before appearing before the Essex Assizes at Chelmsford in July 1849. Palmer confessed to the crime, but Goody denied the charge of 'comforting and assisting' Palmer in the commission of a crime. Goody had originally been charged with burglary, but this had been thrown out by the Grand Jury. Witnesses on his behalf gave evidence that he was with them on the night of the burglary. He was acquitted of the charge, but not before the learned judge said that it would have been pertinent had Goody been charged with burglary.

A death mask - made of plaster - was made of Green. To this day it can still be found on the wall of Strethall Hall, another is in the museum at Saffron Walden.

Five

ARSENIC: THE
INHERITANCE POWDER

Arsenic became a favourite murder weapon of the Middle Ages and Renaissance period, particularly among the ruling classes in Italy. Lucrezia Borgia is perhaps the name people most readily associate with arsenical murder, though it was actually her brother Cesare who was the guilty party. In the seventeenth century a Sicilian woman named Giulia Tofana or Toffana (died 1659) was thought to have killed up to 600 people with a special preparation she sold to women eager to rid themselves of the men in their lives.

Arsenic had acquired the nickname the 'inheritance powder' because impatient heirs were known or suspected to use it to ensure or accelerate their inheritance prospects. Because the symptoms were similar to those of cholera, which was common at the time, arsenic poisoning often went undetected. During the nineteenth century in England, the most famous killer was Mary Ann Cotton, a former Sunday school teacher from County Durham, who, between the early 1860s and her execution in 1873, used arsenic to murder her mother, three husbands, her lodger and most of her fifteen children and stepchildren. In nearly every instance, she was the beneficiary of an insurance policy.

By the 1800s, most arsenical homicides however were committed by the labouring classes. For wives seeking widowhood, arsenic had many advantages. The popularity of arsenic as a murder weapon lay in the fact that it has no taste or colour, and in its powdered form, known as 'white arsenic', it could easily be passed off as sugar, flour or baking powder. Accidental deaths from arsenic greatly outnumbered those from homicide and suicide. Arsenic was an ingredient in Victorian fly papers; soaked in water, it would combine with the water to create a deadly liquid that was easily disguisable in beverages and food. It was also used in rat poison and insecticides, and could be easily bought over the counter at any chemist or grocery store. Victorian women also used a mixture of vinegar, chalk and arsenic to whiten their skin. This use of arsenic was intended to prevent aging and creasing of the skin, but some arsenic was inevitably absorbed into the bloodstream.

This cartoon from *Punch Magazine* shows the Victorian attitude to poisons. It reads:

Mrs Higgins (who has been about half an hour purchasing two pennyworth of poison for rats): 'And how did you say, Mr Killemorph, as how it was to be applied?'

Chemist (absent-mindedly): 'Give' em a teaspoonful after each meal mum.'

As little as a hundredth of an ounce was enough to cause death. Symptoms of arsenic poisoning included extreme stomach pains and cramp, and doctors would often diagnose arsenic poisoning as gastric fever and other causes of natural death. Normally, by the time doctors established the true cause, it was too late for the victim. Inquests were rare, since Justices of the Peace were unwilling to squander public funds on them, so the chances of detection remained small.

There were tests for arsenic dating back to the 1700s, but they were unreliable. However, a reliable method came along during the 1830s, with the introduction of the Marsh test (named after the English chemist James Marsh). The test made it easier to detect murder, and as a result there was a slow decrease in arsenic's use.

The advent of the life insurance industry brought a new motive for murder. Poor families could enrol their children in 'burial clubs' for a halfpenny a week, and if the child died the club would pay as much as £5 towards funeral expenses. With a cheap funeral costing as little as £1, this left a useful surplus for feeding the remaining children. Enterprising families enrolled each child in several clubs to increase the payout.

The burial club scandal became so widespread that in 1850 a law was introduced to prohibit insuring children under the age of ten for more than £3. But this did not deter resolute killers. The lure of life insurance was a motivation for Mary Ann Cotton, who became the most prolific British serial killer on record prior to Harold Shipman in the 1990s.

In Essex, there were a number of murders where arsenic was used. Two in particular stand out.

The Harwich Death Club

Thirty-eight-year-old Mary May lived in the village of Wix, a few miles outside Harwich, with her second husband Robert, and two children, a boy from her first marriage and a boy of 2 by her current husband.

Mary and her husband earned their living by selling bread and other foodstuffs, and shared their house with two lodgers; one was Mary's half-brother William Constable, known locally as Spratty Watts, the other was James Simpson. Spratty had lodged with her for two years and witnesses said that they got on well.

There existed, in Harwich, a burial club, and Mary had joined, insuring her half-brother's life without telling him or her husband, and she stood to receive £10 on his death – a considerable sum when you consider that a farm labourer's wage at the time was seven or eight shillings a week. Mary had falsified her age and that of her half-brother when registering with the club.

Mary had every opportunity to poison Spratty. He was, after all, living in the same house and she cooked meals for him, which they ate together. There was also evidence that she had tried to buy arsenic, although there appears to be no evidence that she actually possessed any. No containers in the house were analysed for traces of the poison.

Watts became ill on Thursday, 8 June 1848. He was violently sick through the night and into Friday. On the Saturday, Dr William Thompson from Manningtree was called in, and 'found him in great exhaustion'. Watts had previously been supplied with medicine by his assistant

Martin Perry, who had not visited Watts, but had sent the medicine from the surgery at Manningtree.

Watts died on the following Sunday and Mary May went immediately to a near neighbour, and fellow member of the burial club, Susannah Forster for written confirmation of his death so that she might draw the money due for his funeral. The speed with which she made her application following his death, and which had followed so rapidly after the insurance was taken out, were to be strong points in persuading the jury of her guilt.

Nineteen days after Watts' death, on 30 June, Dr Thompson carried out a post-mortem examination. He sent the stomach and its contents to Professor Taylor, who gave evidence that he found 10 grains of arsenic in the contents, 'three being enough to kill a man'.

James Simpson, who shared a room with Watts, told the court about a conversation that Mary had had with him about her membership of the burial club at the time of Watts' final illness and also, in a much more incriminating vein, that she had said, 'please God took him away, she should have £10 out, and get a suit of mourning and bury him respectable, and if she had any money to spare, she would get a donkey and cart.'

The only direct evidence of Mary May actually administering any substance to food ingested by Watts, was the statement given by her own 10-year-old son, William Everett, who said that he saw his mother '(take) something from a paper which she put into the porter, and after boiling it gave it to Watts, but I did not see him drink it.' He also told the court, 'The powder was a white colour, and I have heard Mother call it soda. She had put it into the beer many times before'.

After a long and somewhat impassioned speech from her defence counsel, it took just twenty minutes for the jury to find Mary guilty of killing Watts. In passing sentence of death, the judge told her to, 'make use of the short time that may remain to you here to make your peace with the God that you have offended'. Mary May replied, 'I did not do it, I am innocent.'

Mary was hanged at Chelmsford Gaol in 1848. Her last words to the large crowd which had gathered at her execution were, 'Goodbye, may the Lord have mercy on my soul.' Around 3,000 people turned up to witness her execution and to the end she maintained her innocence.

The subject of burial clubs reached the House of Lords in March 1850, when the Lord Monteagle said:

> …would take that opportunity of asking a question of the noble Marquess (the Marquess of Lansdowne) regarding the laws affecting burial societies. Nothing could be more painful than to see by the reports of the proceedings in our criminal courts, the vast increase of crimes of a most horrible nature – domestic murders, poisonings, and other violent deaths, inflicted by persons between whom and their victims ties of the most tender and the closest nature existed; and it was most shocking to observe that these crimes were perpetrated chiefly in those districts in which burial clubs or societies existed, by the present rules and arrangements of which a pecuniary interest was given to some members of families on the decease of others. He trusted those dreadful crimes and their origin had attracted the attention of Her Majesty's Government, and that some remedy would be applied as soon as possible. He believed that a simple enactment, which

need not cover more than a sheet of note paper, providing that the duty of burial should be performed by those clubs for their members, instead of giving any money upon death taking place, would amply suffice to meet the exigencies of the case; and he wished to know whether any such measure was in contemplation, as, if it were not, he would himself take the liberty of introducing one?

At about the time Mary was using arsenic, a more sinister set of events was taking place on the other side of the county, in the village of Clavering, which led to the deaths of four people.

Sally Arsenic

Sarah Parker was born in Clavering on 9 July 1809. She was married in 1829 to Richard Chesham, a farm labourer who also lived in the village. Clavering was a rural parish in the north-west of the county, some four miles from Newport. Already pregnant at the time of her marriage, she gave birth to a daughter, Harriet, in February 1829, and was to give birth to five more children, all boys, by the time she had reached 30: Philip (born January 1830), John (born November 1832), Joseph (born November 1834), James (born 1837),

and George (born May 1839). The 1841 census shows that the family were living in a cottage at Ponds End, Clavering.

In the autumn of 1847, Sarah was arrested on a charge of poisoning the illegitimate daughter of Lydia Taylor, a servant to the mother of Thomas Newport, a farmer from Clavering, who it was suggested was the father of the child. Together with Newport she was committed for trial. Suspicion also fell on the unexplained deaths of two of her sons, James and Joseph, who had both died in distressing circumstances. The coroner became involved and ordered a post-mortem on the bodies of the two boys, which was carried out by a Professor Taylor from Guys Hospital. Traces of arsenic were found in both. Sarah was arrested and charged with their murder. She appeared before the Assize court at Chelmsford in spring 1848 and, although evidence

Clavering village sign.

was given that the boys had both died from arsenic poisoning, the evidence against Sarah was thin and she was acquitted by the jury, who believed her protestations of innocence. The case involving Taylor's daughter was not proceeded with. The girl subsequently died but there was no proof that she had died from poisoning. Both Sally and Newport were released.

The Times newspaper, referring to Sarah, said that she was, 'an accepted and reputed murderess who walked abroad in a village unchallenged and unaccused, and . . . all the inhabitants had seen her children buried without remark or outcry, though they were clearly convinced that there had been foul play.'

Sarah continued to live in Clavering, where three years later, in May 1850, her husband Richard died after an illness lasting three or four months. He was buried at the age of 43 at Clavering church. Described by neighbours as a generally fit person, Richard suffered from a lung disease, with intermittent bouts of violent pain and sickness, and it was not long before neighbours in the village began to speculate that Sarah had been up to her old tricks again and poisoned him. The coroner was alerted and the contents of Richard's stomach were analysed. Tiny traces of arsenic were found in his body, but not enough to suggest that his wife had helped him on his way.

The police interviewed a friend of Sarah's, Hannah Phillips. The two women were much maligned by the villagers, who dubbed them both 'Sally Arsenic'. There was nothing to prove against them, however – or at least there wasn't until the two women fell out. Hannah told the police about a conversation she had had with Sarah, in which she (Hannah) spoke of her own unhappy marriage. Sarah, she alleged, had said, 'I wouldn't live with such a man.' And then she gave Hannah some advice, suggesting she ought to do what she had done, make him up a pie of sheep's liver, lights, etc., and that if she brought it to her she would season it for her.

On hearing the new evidence, Superintendent John Clarke, of the Essex Constabulary, immediately obtained a warrant for Sarah's arrest and she was taken to Newport police station, where she was interviewed. Clarke then searched her house and removed a bag of rice, which, when analysed at Guys Hospital, was found to have arsenic mixed with it. Sarah again protested her innocence, blaming the arsenic in her husband's body on the medicine he was taking.

Sarah appeared before the Chelmsford Assizes in March 1851, on a charge of administering poison with intent. The jury this time had no hesitation in finding her guilty and she was sentenced to death. She was hanged on Tuesday, 25 March 1851, outside Chelmsford Prison before a crowd of 7,000, the last woman to be executed in Britain for attempted murder. She shared the scaffold with Samuel Drory, who had been convicted of the murder of his pregnant girlfriend.

As Sarah had not been hanged for murder, but rather administering poison with intent, her body was released from the prison and returned to Clavering for burial. The *Chelmsford Chronicle* reported on 4 April 1851 that the body had been returned with the noose still around the neck, although this was strenuously denied by the prison authorities. Sarah's burial took place in Clavering churchyard at seven o'clock in the evening and was watched by around 150 spectators. However it is reported that there was no religious service and there is no entry in the burial register.

Due to the number of arsenic homicide cases in England during the nineteenth century, the government introduced the 1851 Sale of Arsenic Act, which forbade the sale of arsenic compounds unless the purchaser was known to the pharmacist. Moreover, manufacturers were required to mix each pound of arsenic powder with one ounce of colouring (soot or indigo), which further made it difficult for people to slip arsenic into food and beverages.

Six

THE SIBLE HEDINGHAM
WITCHCRAFT CASE

Throughout Europe during the sixteenth and seventeenth centuries, many thousands of innocent people were killed in the hunt for witches. In 1584, Pope Paul VIII issued an edict which made witchcraft a heresy and torture was used as a means of extracting 'confessions'. Between 1560 and 1680 in Essex alone 317 women and twenty-three men were tried for witchcraft, and over 100 were hanged. In 1645 there were thirty-six witch trials in Essex, leading to eight women at Manningtree and nineteen women at Chelmsford being condemned to the gallows.

The man responsible was Matthew Hopkins, a little known lawyer practising in Manningtree in north Essex, who, in 1644, published a book entitled *Discovery of Witches*. Hopkins travelled throughout the Eastern Counties in his quest for witches, becoming known as the 'Witchfinder General'. Hopkins, with his assistant John Stearne, toured the villages of Essex, investigating accusations of witchcraft. In little more than a year, they accused over 100 elderly, poor, lonely women of witchcraft – women who had no one to defend them. It is believed that Hopkins received a fee for every witch who was hanged, and that he may have had up to 400 people hanged; a lucrative business.

There is some dispute as to how Hopkins met his end. Some accounts say he was himself hanged as a witch, while it is believed he died of consumption in Mistley in 1647.

The last execution for witchcraft in England took place in 1682, and the last trial in 1712. The law was repealed in 1736.

One of the preferred methods of determining the guilt of a witch was known as 'swimming', where the victim, right thumb tied to left toe, was thrown into water. If the poor soul sank they were declared innocent, whether they drowned or not, but if they floated then they were definitely a witch and met their death at the stake.

The ordeal of 'swimming' was endorsed by James I of England, who stated in *Daemonologie* (1597) 'that God hath appointed ... that the water shall refuse to receive them

Matthew Hopkins, Witchfinder General.

in her bosome, that have shaken off them the sacred Water of Baptisme, and wilfully refused the benefite thereof.'

By 1863, Queen Victoria had been on the throne for twenty-six years; the first underground railway was opened in London, whilst in America, the Civil War had been waging for two years. The Battle of Gettysburg had been fought, leaving over 40,000 dead in the cornfields and orchards of the small Pennsylvania township, and in rural Essex the village of Sible Hedingham was to become the scene of what is regarded by many as the last case of witchcraft to occur in this country.

By the nineteenth century, attitudes had changed. Superstitious people still believed in witchcraft and those suspected of being witches were treated as outsiders and often avoided by other villagers. However in 1863, an elderly man died as a consequence of the shock of being 'swum in water' as a witch and two persons appeared in court in connection with his death.

The facts of the case are simple. Sible Hedingham, a large scattered village of some 1,800 inhabitants, consisted mainly of agricultural labourers, with some tradesmen. The victim was an elderly man, by common consent a Frenchman, although it had to be admitted nothing was known of his nationality. He was deaf and dumb and at the time of his death was estimated to be between 80 and 86 years of age. Nothing definite was known about his past, but it was rumoured that he had had his tongue cut out by the Chinese whilst fighting for the French. This led to his nickname – 'Dummy'. He lived in a wretched mud hut on the outskirts of the village for several years and was a figure of curiosity. Always accompanied by several dogs, he wore several hats of different descriptions, all at the same time, and as many as three coats, depending on the weather at the time. Unable to speak, he communicated by means of signs and gesticulated in a vivacious and excitable fashion. He gained a living by telling fortunes, in the main feeding on the superstitions of the local populace.

The scene of the tragedy was The Swan public house, which stood in the centre of the village and was a popular resort for the local populace to while away an evening. Nearby ran a shallow brook, no more than a few feet deep, in which the 'swimming' was to take place.

On the evening of 3 August, Dummy was to be found as usual in the tap room of The Swan. There were between forty and fifty other people in the premises, including 36-year-old Emma Smith, the wife of the beerhouse keeper at nearby Ridgewell. She was an emotional, excitable and highly-strung woman, and also very superstitious. Also present was Samuel Stammers, a 28-year-old master carpenter by trade, who lived in the village.

Sible Hedingham village sign.

Smith complained in a loud voice that she had been ill for some nine to ten months and that her illness was caused by Dummy, who had bewitched her. She begged him to return with her to her home in the village of Ridgewell, a few miles distance of Hedingham, and remove the curse. So desperate was she that she offered him three gold sovereigns; but Dummy was having none of it, fearing that his life would be in danger if he went with her. She continued to plead with him, much to the amusement of the assembled audience, who, sensing more fun, continued to encourage Smith. At closing time the action moved to outside the public house, where Smith, still encouraged by the crowd, which had now grown to about eighty people, continued to plead with Dummy.

Eventually, seeing she was getting nowhere, she tore the old man's coat and struck him several times over the arms and shoulders with a stick and kicked him and dragged him down to the brook near the Swan. Pushing him in, she said, 'you old devil you served me out, now I will serve you out.' Dummy tried to get out of the brook by the opposite side, but was prevented by Smith, who had rushed round to cut off his exit. At this point Stammers appears to have joined in and the pair pushed the unfortunate man once more into the brook. Dummy managed to struggle out of the water and sat exhausted on the bank.

Smith and Stammers once again took hold of the old man and threw him back into the water, where he struggled. The mood of the bystanders, who had until this time been encouraging the pair and assisting with a barrage of stones, now began to change as they became alarmed at what was going on. One shouted, 'If someone does not take the old man out, he will die in a moment.' Stammers, perhaps coming to his senses, jumped into the brook and pulled the old man out on to the bank. Dummy was assisted back to his home, where he was left. The next day he was visited by Mr Fowke, one of the Guardians of the Poor of that parish, who found him in a terrible state, still wet and trembling violently and very badly bruised.

He was in much pain and screamed loudly when his wet clothes were taken from him. Superintendent Thomas Elsey of the Essex Constabulary was informed and had Dummy removed to the Halstead Workhouse, where he died on 4 September, of pneumonia brought upon by the immersion and ill treatment.

The Swan public house.

The brook next to The Swan, where 'the
swimming' took place. The brook has
been much altered over the past 150 years.

The police, under the direction of Superintendent Jeremiah Raison, began an investigation into the events of 3 August and on 25 September, Smith and Stammers were charged by Elsey, before the magistrates at Castle Hedingham, with having 'unlawfully assaulted an old Frenchman commonly called Dummy, thereby causing his death.' The case had attracted much interest and the small courtroom was packed. Witnesses to the events were reluctant to give evidence against Smith and Stammers, but several told the court the facts as related above. Mr Sinclair, a surgeon to the Halstead workhouse, said that death was due to the treatment the old man had received. Smith and Stammers were both committed to the next sitting of the Assize court at Chelmsford.

On 8 March 1864, the two accused stood next to each other in the dock. They pleaded not guilty. Smith told the court that the deceased had come to her house, had spat at her and told her that after a time she would become ill, and she was ill. She had called a doctor twice in one night and he could not cure her. Dummy, she told the court, made her ill and bewitched her. A telling witness against the two accused was 10-year-old Eva Henrietta Garrad, described as a child of precocious intelligence. Despite her tender years she unfolded in clear terms the events of the night to the court. The defence made strenuous efforts to discredit her, but her evidence was enough to place the guilt of Smith and Stammers beyond doubt. Much was made of the mental state of Smith and the fact that Stammers had pulled the old man out of the water. The judge, Sir William Erle, took these factors into account when he sentenced both defendants to six months' hard labour.

Was Dummy a witch? Certainly he played on the superstitions of the local people. He was consulted by the local girls as a recognised authority on courtship and marriage; and when police searched his home they found numerous scraps of paper with various queries written on them. One such query read, 'Her husband have left her many years, and she want to know whether he is dead or alive.' Even 130 years ago, in rural Essex, the fear of witchcraft was a firmly held belief in the minds of country people.

Seven

THE COGGESHALL GANG

An early test of the resolve and determination of the Essex Constabulary came just a few years after its formation in 1840. Coggeshall was in the Witham Division under the command of Superintendent Charles Cooke, who had just two constables at Witham and two constables stationed at Coggeshall to deal with matters brought to their attention.

For some time past the neighbourhood of Coggeshall had been plagued by a gang of housebreakers, who, according to the *Essex Standard* in June 1838, 'have carried out their work in a most audacious manner.'

Between 1844 and 1848, a series of violent crimes took place in Coggeshall and the surrounding villages, which had the local inhabitants in fear for their safety. A group of up to fourteen men, known locally as the Coggeshall Gang, carried out the crimes. They had their headquarters at the Black Horse Inn, in Stonegate Street, the landlord of which was William French, the half-brother of the leader of the gang, Samuel Crow. French benefited from the proceeds of the crimes by receiving stolen property from the gang. Crow was employed in driving post-chaises for innkeepers and gentry and was well known in the neighbourhood.

Armed with pistols and cudgels and wearing masks, the gang operated mainly at night and terrorised the local inhabitants.

The first offence occurred in November 1844, when the unoccupied home of a Mr Charles Skingsley in Coggeshall was broken into, a quantity of wines stolen and the house burnt down. In 1845 two burglaries were reported, one at the Bird in Hand public house in East Street, and another in February 1845, at the warehouse of grocer Richard Bell. The proceeds of this crime consisted of eight hams worth £10, a quantity of bacon, 27lb in weight of candles and about seventeen cakes of soap. In 1847 another burglary took place and in 1848 no fewer than seven were reported to the police. It is possible that other offences went unreported.

In March 1848, at Bradwell, four members of the gang entered a house and terrorised the occupants, 62-year-old James Finch and his housekeeper Elizabeth Wright for nearly three hours. During this time, they were both held over an open fire to reveal where money was hidden and Elizabeth Wright was seriously injured when her clothes ignited. James Finch was also dragged upstairs, a rope tied round his neck, and he was hoisted up to a beam. The gang helped themselves to food and drink, which they consumed on the premises. In addition to £6 in monies they stole four hams, two pig's faces and half the contents of a tub of pork, all of which they carried away in a sack and basket.

In another raid that year the gang entered a house and threatened the frightened householder with a pistol. They then put a mattress on him onto which they piled furniture and boxes, almost suffocating the poor man. The gang remained in the house for several hours, during which time they consumed several bottles of wine before leaving with £5 in gold and silver.

The local police force found it difficult to catch the gang, but in 1847, one gang member, William Wade, had been caught through the efforts of one constable, and at the Summer Assizes in that year was sentenced to be transported for fifteen years. While in Chelmsford Prison he was visited by Samuel Crow, who promised to look after Wade's wife if he kept quiet, but the gang failed to honour this agreement and the furious Wade informed the Governor of the prison of the identity of the other gang members.

The Magistrates at Witham were informed and warrants were issued for the arrest of William 'Crusty' Ellis, William Springett, William Tansley and Samuel Crow. Springett, a thatcher by trade, was arrested at Feering; Tansley, a labourer, was found at Meeting Street, Coggeshall, and soon they were lodged in Chelmsford Gaol. Two further members of the gang, William Payne and Thomas Whittaker, had escaped to Liverpool, where they were apprehended on board a ship bound for New York, the two men being taken off the ship and placed in chains. Both men were taken back to Witham but were later acquitted. The arrests were made by PC Charles Livermore, who had travelled from Witham to Liverpool for that purpose. 'Crusty' Ellis had also made good his escape and it wasn't until October 1848 that he was finally captured in Bury St Edmunds by PC Charles Kerridge.

Superintendent Cooke, together with Inspector Ward and Constables Smith and Nicholls, went to the Black Horse Inn in search of Crow, and questioned French, who denied any knowledge of his whereabouts. A search was made of the premises but they failed to find Crow. The constables were left to watch over the premises and later that night a search was made of a house in the yard of the Black Horse, where it was suspected Crow may be hiding.

During the search, PC Nicholls found a hole in a ceiling, covered by a piece of board. Climbing up to investigate he discovered Crow sitting on a beam near the chimney. Crow offered to surrender and Nicholls, lowering himself down to call for help, gave Crow the opportunity to make a dash for freedom. Crow clambered over several roof tops, dropped down from a 12ft wall, scaled another 10ft high and escaped to Abbey Mill, where he remained hidden until his brother, John, aged 15, came in a gig owned by French and collected him. Avoiding the tollgates they made their way via a circuitous route to Brentwood, where Samuel Crow was left. A reward of £20 was offered for his arrest.

Crow made his way to London, having booked a ticket on a steamer, the *James Watt*, bound for Hamburg. Unfortunately for him, a Metropolitan police officer 'generally employed in detective service' named Joseph Puddifoot was on his trail and, having studied his picture in the 'Hue and Cry', made his move. On 26 October, the day the boat was due to leave, Puddifoot, accompanied by Sergeant Thomas Pearson, went aboard the *James Watt* and picked out their man, fashionably dressed, though 'the style of the stable still predominated'. Crow again attempted to escape but was unsuccessful.

The trial of the gang took place at the Essex Lent Assizes at Chelmsford on the first Monday in March 1849, the Right Honourable Sir James Parke, Kt., presiding. The public galleries were 'filled to suffocation by respectfully dressed females.' William Wade, who had turned Queen's evidence, was to be the star witness, but not before Parke warned the jury that his evidence must be treated with caution. Details of the trial were reported in the *Chelmsford Chronicle*.

The first case to be heard by the jury involved the burglary at Bradwell and three defendants, William Tansley, William Ellis, and Samuel Crow were indicted for the crime. Appearing in the dock with them were William French and John Crow, who were indicted for harbouring and assisting the escape of Samuel Crow. The prosecution case took six hours and relied upon the evidence of Wade, who was present during the burglary, and the identification of Crow by James Finch. The jury took only twelve minutes to reach a verdict and they acquitted Ellis and Tansley.

Other charges were heard, involving various defendants, and included burglaries at Little Coggeshall, Cressing and Great Tey, larceny at the warehouse of Mr Bell at Coggeshall and highway robbery of a Mr Richard Dell, a Miller at Feering in October 1847.

At the end of the trial, those of the gang who had been found guilty were sentenced for their part in the crimes. Samuel Crow, Tansley and Ellis were each sentenced to be transported for life. In sentencing Ellis, the judge said:

> For the part you have taken in this guilty transaction in robbing and injuring Mr Dell, your life is forfeited to the laws of your country, and if I did choose to interfere by recommending you to the merciful consideration of Her Majesty, the consequences would be that you would suffer an ignominious death. You have been evidently not concerned in this alone; but the circumstances of the injury to the prosecutor were not so great as to justify me in letting the sentence take its course, therefore your life will be spared, but the rest of it will be spent abroad.

Everett and French were sentenced to be transported for seven years and John Crow received three months' hard labour for assisting his brother to escape. Samuel Crow never served his sentence – he died in Chelmsford Prison in March 1850. Two other gang members were also transported for seven years.

Wade, who had been an active member of the gang, had his sentence reduced to transportation for seven years and thus ended the reign of terror that the Coggeshall Gang had brought to this quiet part of rural Essex.

Eight

BODY SNATCHERS

Between the fifteenth and the early nineteenth centuries, the only legal source of corpses for dissection in England was from executed criminals. However, not enough bodies were provided to supply the increasing number of anatomy schools being opened and their burgeoning numbers of students. To supply this demand, body snatchers (also known as grave-robbers or resurrectionists) would obtain fresh corpses from the graves of those recently buried.

A Select Committee on Anatomy recommended the requisition of the bodies of individuals dying in workhouses or hospitals, too poor to pay for their own funerals. Despite opposition, these findings were eventually embodied in the Anatomy Act of 1832, which allowed the unclaimed bodies of institutionalized paupers to be sold to anatomy schools for dissection.

In December 1823, the residents of Little Leighs, near Chelmsford, witnessed the real horrors involved in the crime of body snatching. This was a crime mostly experienced in the metropolis but as security in the graveyards there increased, the resurrectionists had to travel further afield to carry out their gruesome trade.

The unguarded churchyards of villages, such as that at Little Leighs, became perfect targets. The crimes that took place here are well recorded. The depositions of the witnesses still exist, as do the press cuttings of the time and, thanks to the incompetence of the criminal, the chain of events that took place in Little Leighs can be plotted.

Little Leighs has changed very little since the early nineteenth century so it is quite easy to establish where the events took place. The village is to the south-west of Great Leighs, and lies between Braintree to the north and Broomfield and Chelmsford to the south. The road that joins them is an old Roman road now better known as the A131. At Little Leighs, in 1823, there was a tollgate across this road. Although not the busiest of the Essex turnpikes, this road still carried a fair amount of traffic. From the turnpike there is a junction with a road running westwards, now known as Church Lane, although at the time it was unnamed. About half a mile along this road, on the left, is St John's Church with its graveyard, the scene of the crime.

Other important locations are the field with a gate at the junction of Church Lane and the turnpike. From the tithe map of 1838 we know it was called Lower Reedings and next to that, along Church Lane, is another field called Church Brooms. About half a mile from the tollgate and travelling along the turnpike towards Braintree is St Anne's Castle public house.

In 1823, nine residents from Little Leighs were buried in the churchyard. This was a high number for a small village with a population of 160. Three were buried in December. The first of the three was Susannah Knight, aged 30, who was buried on the 14th. The following day Abraham Leader, aged 33, was buried, and on 21 December Johanna Chinnery, aged 24, was buried. We know from the church records that Johanna had a baby daughter, Mary, whilst still unmarried. The child was baptised on 29 July 1822.

The records show that having children out of wedlock was not uncommon. However, Johanna married James Chinnery a year later, on 16 July 1823. Alas, this was to be a tragically short marriage for five months later she was dying.

We know from the *Chelmsford Chronicle* that, just prior to her death, she requested which clothes she should be buried in. James granted her this wish for he stated that she was buried wearing a shift, gown, night-cap and a pair of white cotton stockings. The local carpenter, Joseph White, confirmed this as he made her coffin and screwed the lid down.

What follows is taken from the *Chelmsford Chronicle*, and the initial depositions. Around 5 o'clock in the morning of Friday 26 December, Charles Rogers of Fairsted was walking home from Felsted. Being a superstitious man, he did not walk through St John's churchyard but made a detour and came across a horse cart in the field called Lower Reedings.

The horse was tied to a tree by a whip. Finding no owner, he told the toll collector, John Redwood, what he had found. Redwood went to the field with him and saw that the cart contained an umbrella, a pair of dirty pantaloons and food for both the horse and driver.

The two men took the horse and gig to St Anne's Castle public house and handed them to the landlord, John Crisp, for safekeeping. They told him of the circumstances in which they had been found and that if someone came to claim them they should not be handed back unless they gave a good account of themselves. This was about 5 or 6 o'clock in the morning.

About two hours later, Crisp was with another man called Francis when they were approached by a man named Samuel Clark. Clark asked after the horse and gig. He told John Crisp that he got tipsy overnight by drinking ale and eating toast. He tied his horse to a tree in a field and lay down to sleep it off. When he awoke, he found the horse and cart gone. Crisp, being satisfied with that explanation, handed the cart over to him. Clark paid for the hay and said he was going to meet a Mr Jay from Cavendish, and headed off towards Braintree.

John Broomfield, the local blacksmith, lived near the tollgate and heard of the unusual happenings the previous night and, out of curiosity, went to Lower Reedings to see what he could find. There he found a shovel on the branch of a tree. He then went to the next field, Church Brooms, and found a sack, doubled up, upon which were printed in red letters the words 'J. Harvey, Crayford Mill'.

St John's Church in Little Leighs, where the
body of Johanna Chinnery was taken from.

When he lifted the sack a brace of pistols fell out. He then went to find the owner
of the land – Hugh Simons of Leighs Hall – who was also the churchwarden. Simons
returned with Broomfield to the spot where the sack was found and began searching the
ditch. About 12ft away he found a woman's body, partly covered with earth. Fearing that a
murder had been committed, he went to get help.

On his way he passed the churchyard, where he found that the earth on Johanna
Chinnery's grave had been disturbed and that her burial clothes had been strewn around.
The events then became clear to him. One can only assume that they went to the St Anne's
Castle to see if the owner of the horse and gig had turned up. They were too late – Clark
had already gone. One can only assume that what followed was a hue and cry to catch him.

The story of his capture is gleaned from the newspaper account. It seems that when
Clark left the St Anne's Castle he went north towards Braintree. However, he soon turned
off and took a circuitous route back to the Chelmsford road to avoid the tollgate. He had
left his horse and cart at Cottee's the blacksmith and was found drinking at the King's
Arms public house, Broomfield. He must have thought he had got away with it. On being
questioned, Clark denied any knowledge of the pistols and stuck to his story.

John Broomfield remembered seeing Clark drinking with another man at the St Anne's
Castle on Wednesday 17 December. This man was not found. Clark said that he was a
dealer by trade. He recalled that he had been to prison but had overlooked the fact that he
had been to the pillory for selling a sick horse. He claimed he lived at Haggerstone Bridge,
where the police officer there testified that Clark was of an indifferent character who
annoyed the neighbours and carried out his dealings mostly at night.

On the order of a magistrate on Wednesday 31 December, the churchyard of St John's
was again visited and the graves of Abraham Leader and Susannah Knight were dug up.
Their coffins were opened and found to be empty except for the shrouds, which had
been stripped from the bodies. The newspaper is very unkind about Susannah Knight
by posthumously accusing her of being responsible for much vice in the parish of Little
Leighs and, unsurprisingly, met an early death. Sensationalism sold newspapers then as
now. Clark was charged with taking these bodies as well as that of Johanna Chinnery.
He was also accused of stealing the clothes she was buried in.

Justice could be swift in those days for Clark appeared before the court on Friday,
23 January 1824. The case was reported in the *Chelmsford Chronicle*. Little in the way

of new facts arose except that the pistols were found to be loaded. The prosecution opened the case with the most lurid account, making out that the accused was the darkest of characters. Considering the facts of the case, even the reporter could not add more to that.

In his defence Clark denied everything. Oddly, much was reported on the defence's case for not stealing the clothes. Clarke's counsel made clear that whoever stripped them off the body had shown no intention of anything other than leaving them there and in that case the defendant should not be found guilty. There may be a case to make today but the prosecution successfully countered this defence and Clark was found guilty of stealing the burial clothes of Johanna Chinnery. He was sentenced to be transported for seven years. He continued to protest his innocence. The three indictments of taking the bodies had no evidence presented and therefore not guilty verdicts were recorded.

There is no record of the bodies of Abraham Leader or Susannah Knight ever being recovered. As for Johanna Chinnery, she was reburied and, this time, stayed that way. As for her widower, James, in July 1825, a year later, there is recorded a baptism of John, son to James and Pricilla Chinnery. Life was possibly too short to remain unmarried for long.

The case presents some questions to which, after nearly 200 years, there are few answers. Was Clark justified to protest his innocence? One cannot help but believe the outcome of the court case was the right one. He did not deny that the horse and cart were his. They were found in a field adjacent to the body, which was lying in a field next but one to the churchyard. In effect they were in a straight line. He was never able to provide a satisfactory account of his actions for Christmas day and the night that followed. Did he take the other two bodies? Probably not. The disturbance of their graves had gone unnoticed and the shrouds had been put back in the graves. Altogether a much more accomplished crime.

The taking of Johanna Chinnery was, by any standards, a shambles. It is difficult to conceive of a more amateurish job. It is likely that the person who was with Clark in the St Anne's Castle pub the week prior to the theft was responsible for taking the first two bodies and was showing Clark where it was done. He had not chosen his accomplice well. The final question remains that, as a result of the resurrectionists, how many graves are still, in fact, lying empty?

Another case had occurred two years previously, in November 1821, involving an infamous gang of resurrectionists who were apprehended whilst operating far from their usual London haunts by a brave village constable, James Adlam, parish constable of Abridge. Adlam had gone to the Blue Boar public house in Abridge at about nine o'clock, having heard rumours there were two men there with a horse and cart who had been seen acting suspiciously. The cart was outside and Adlam saw the name of the owner of the cart was a William Hollis of Thomas Street, Newington, Surrey. The two men left the public house and got in the cart and drove off in the direction of Ongar. The constable went to get his mare with the intention of following the men but before he could do so, the cart returned with a third man, travelling at a rapid speed through the village along the London Road in the direction of Chigwell.

Adlam gave chase but he did not catch up with the cart until it had reached Chigwell. When he did manage to stop it there were now four men in the cart. He took two men into custody but in the scuffle the other two escaped. The men detained were William and James Crouch.

On searching the cart Adlam found the body of a female child, which was later identified as that of Sarah Barker, the 8-year-old daughter of William Barker, the shoemaker for Abridge. Sarah had been buried on the Sunday before, in the cemetery in Lambourne. John Jones, the undertaker, stated that on Sunday 28 October last, he conducted the funeral and secured the lid of the coffin knowing she was in it, and saw it placed in the grave in the churchyard.

William Barker went to the Blue Boar and identified the body of his daughter Sarah.

James and William Crouch appeared before the Essex Assizes at Chelmsford in January 1822. They were charged with 'carrying away dead bodies from a grave'. Each received a sentence of three months' imprisonment, which seems nothing to the anguish they caused Sarah's parents.

Nine

THE COLCHESTER
FIRE MURDER

Shortly before 10 p.m. on Friday, 8 December 1893, PC Charles Alexander of the Colchester Borough Police was patrolling his beat in Short Wyre Street, when he noticed flames coming from the premises of Alfred Welch, tailor and outfitter. Sounding the alarm, fire engines from the Essex and Suffolk Insurance Company and the Volunteer Fire Brigade, supervised by the Chief Constable and Firemaster R.O. Coombes, were soon tackling the blaze. Quick work by the two fire brigades managed to contain the fire and prevent it spreading to neighbouring premises, but they were unable to save Welch's shop, which was totally destroyed by the fire.

Enquiries were made to trace Alfred Welch, who was known to have been in the building just before 8 o'clock in the evening, when he had returned from London. He had spoken to his foreman, Henry Sizzey, and told him to go home, saying that he had an appointment with a former employee, Arthur Blatch, and that he would lock up the premises when he had finished. Welch told Sizzey that Blatch asked him for a private meeting, saying, 'something terrible is going to happen'. As Blatch's wife had recently left, him Welch thought he would ask for money to go after her, and that 'something dreadful' was going to happen to her.

The seat of the fire was discovered in a workroom above Welch's office and a search made amongst the fire debris revealed the charred remains of a body, lying face down at the foot of the workroom stairs. A closer examination revealed a rope wound around the neck; the arms and legs were burned away and the body scarcely recognisable. Underneath the body were a set of keys, which were identified as the keys to the deed and cashbox. The body also wore the remains of an identifiable truss, which Welch was known to wear. A post-mortem was carried out on the Sunday, by Dr Maybury, the police surgeon, assisted by Dr Becker and Dr Bond, a Home Office expert who had been called in to assist in the case. The skull had been fractured and thus suicide was discounted. Bond's opinion was

Sketch from the *Essex Standard* showing the premises of Alfred Welch.

Sketch from the *Essex Standard* showing where the body was found.

that death followed an extensive skull fracture caused by violent blows to the head with a hammer or an axe-head. Injuries were inconsistent with falling downstairs. The rope had been put around Welch's neck after death to simulate suicide by hanging and the fire started to cover up the crime. Blood was also found on the carpet in Mr Welch's office and it was concluded that Welch had met his death there.

An inquest was opened at the Town Hall, Colchester, before the coroner, Mr A.E. Church, on Saturday 16 December. Identification and cause of death were presented to the court and evidence was also given that a cashbox containing £183 was missing from the premises. The inquest was adjourned for further enquires. Sizzey, who was the last person to see the deceased alive, was initially suspected of the crime, but at the adjourned inquest evidence was heard of efforts to find Arthur Blatch, now the main suspect. It was known that Blatch, who was aged about 35, had been travelling the country as an itinerant photographer (although apparently he knew little about photography), and was believed to be currently touring the 'south coast watering places'. He was believed to be in the company of a young woman named Elizabeth Rash, aged 24. A description of Blatch and Rash were circulated to police forces throughout the country.

Police visited Blatch's home and spoke to his estranged wife, who admitted that her husband had visited her and had hidden in the house for a few days prior to the murder.

Inspector Albert Summons and Detective Sergeant George Alexander were sent to London to continue their enquiries and, with the help of the Metropolitan Police, they went to an address in Titchfield Street, Bloomsbury, where Blatch and Rash had been staying, posing as husband and wife. Mrs Lincoln, the landlady, said Blatch had not been there since going to Colchester in early November, but she later admitted that he had returned at midday on 9 December, paying her outstanding rent of £2 9s in gold and silver. Mrs Lincoln then told an extraordinary story. When Blatch had paid her the outstanding rent, he asked her to say that if anyone called for him to say she had not seen him since November. When asked why, he replied that some of his friends believed him to be insane and wanted him put away.

It later transpired that Blatch was actually in the house on 9 December when Detective Sergeant George Alexander called to serve a summons upon him to attend the inquest. Blatch then left as soon as he was able. Elizabeth Rash was traced to another London address, and was taken to Scotland Yard where she was interviewed. She told police that when he left for Colchester, Blatch only had three pence in his possession. He took with him his camera in a canvas bag and tripod, intending, he told her, to work as a photographer. On his return he was wearing new clothes. He told her he had been in Colchester the whole time and had left on the night of Friday 8 December, walking to Witham to catch a train to London. When she asked him if he had seen Mr Welch, he turned pale at the sound of his name. When he took off his shirt, she saw the cuffs were missing. He explained that he had cut them off because they were dirty. He had then burnt the shirt, although she had not noticed any blood on it. More importantly, Blatch had £80 in sovereigns and half-sovereigns in his possession, but gave no explanation as to how he had come by them. Rash handed police the camera, tripod, canvas bag and overcoat, together with five Trichinopoli cigars of the type Welch was known to keep in his office. She also handed over a cap, which she said Blatch was wearing when he returned from Colchester.

The overcoat was examined by Dr Becker, who found traces of blood in the coat lining. The cap belonged to an employee of Welch. It had been left in the shop on the day of the fire and had not been seen since.

At the adjourned inquest on 21 December, witnesses came forward to give evidence. Blatch had been seen in an agitated state outside the premises just before 8 p.m. on the night of the fire. Another witness saw Welch let him in by a side door, as a foundry whistle blew 8 p.m. A woman living opposite saw a man she could not identify leave at 9.30 p.m. At 10.45 p.m. the licensee of the Swan at Stanway saw a man carrying a tripod and camera, wearing the cap and coat produced to the court. He demanded brandy and tried to avoid being seen. He was blowing as if having walked fast. Two constables, making a midnight conference point at Easthorpe, spoke to a man carrying and wearing the said items. Such a man caught an early train at Witham.

The inquest returned a verdict of wilful murder against Arthur Blatch.

A reward of £50 for his arrest was offered by the Watch Committee and 700 handbills were circulated throughout the United Kingdom and Continent. Shipping offices were alerted. Details appeared in the *Police Gazette*:

Arthur Blatch, also known as George (may have assumed the name Jackson). Aged about thirty-five, five feet eight inches, thin build, narrow chested, pale, sickly complexion, thin face, hollow cheeks, small dark eyes, dark brown hair and moustache, very prominent Adam's apple. Heavy smoker with discoloured teeth. Had suffered spinal injury and stooped a little when walking. Weak on his legs and cannot perform much physical effort. Effeminate voice.

Known to have a violent temper and had often beaten his wife. Enjoyed bagatelle and fishing. Employed by Welch for some years, dismissed for too many absences and waning illness. Later recreational ground keeper for Colchester Council, dismissed as incapable of manual work. Character was said to be good during this time. Also worked as a potman . . .

Sightings of Blatch were investigated and anyone who looked like him was questioned, but for almost seven years nothing was heard. Then, in November 1900, police in Wellington, New Zealand, contacted Colchester Police to the fact that they were holding a man in custody answering the description of Arthur Blatch, having been recognised by ex-Colchester residents living in that country.

Sergeant Robert Frost and the Colchester Town Hall Keeper Mr Marsh, who both knew Blatch very well, were sent to New Zealand to collect him. It should be remembered that in 1901 the only route available was by sea and the journey took several months to complete. At first neither Frost nor Marsh were able to identify him, but gradually they became more certain that the man was indeed Blatch. The prisoner, however, insisted he was not Blatch, but Charles Lillywhite, who had been born in London and had never been to Colchester in his life. He had letters in his possession indicating that from 1885 to 1894 he was resident in Tacoma, Washington State, USA. A photograph was sent to Tacoma and people who knew Lillywhite confirmed his identity. Blatch had a tooth worn away by smoking a pipe, but Lillywhite's teeth were examined and found to be perfect, with no sign of dentistry. Despite this, Frost and Marsh insisted they had their man. Putting him before the court, Wellington magistrates were satisfied and ordered his return, refusing a defence request for a writ of *Habeus Corpus*.

The prisoner, together with Frost and Marsh, sailed for home on 9 March 1901, arriving back on 16 June 1901 and he appeared in court, where he was remanded in custody. Lillywhite's brother and sister tried to identify him but they failed until he shaved off his beard. He continued to maintain that he was not Blatch, and eventually the magistrates were convinced and he was released without charge.

Arthur Blatch was never traced and the case remains open, with the £50 reward still available. Why, in New Zealand, did Frost and Marsh insist that the prisoner was Blatch against all the evidence that was before them? Whether the latter ever returned to New Zealand is not known. Dr Bond, the Home Office expert who had been called in to assist with the post-mortem, committed suicide shortly before Lillywhite reached this country. Suffering from melancholia, he jumped from a third-floor window. Welch's outfitters shop is now a newsagent and confectioners. The upper floor, scene of the murder and arson in 1893, is currently used as a store. There is nothing to indicate the horror that happened there a century ago.

Ten

'I, DONALD HUME, DO HEREBY CONFESS...'

At 12.30 p.m. on 21 October 1949, Stanley Tiffin, a 47-year-old farm labourer from Tillingham, was sailing his punt through the Essex marshes in search of wildfowl, when he landed something altogether more macabre.

Spotting a grey bundle floating in the sea, which looked like bedding tied together with string, he scooped it out of the water and undid it. As he did so, part of a man's torso, minus the head and legs, floated out. Tiffen secured the body to a stake to prevent the remains floating out to sea on the tide and sailed back to Tillingham, where he reported his grizzly find to the police.

The torso was removed to St John's Hospital in Chelmsford, where a post-mortem examination was carried out by Dr Francis Camps, the Home Office pathologist. Camps concluded that death was due to stab wounds to the chest, caused by a two-edged sharp weapon about an inch wide at its maximum. The body was clothed in a silk shirt and vest, and a pair of braces, to which were attached part of a pair of trousers. Camps was also able to say that the head and legs had been removed after death by a sharp instrument. He also added another clue – the torso appeared to have been dropped from a great height.

Even without the benefit of DNA testing, it didn't take long to identify the unfortunate victim. Detectives were in luck. Whoever had dismembered the corpse had not removed the arms – making fingerprint identification a formality. Fingerprint experts were called in and leading Scotland Yard expert, Fred Cherrill, took some of the wrinkled skin from the fingers of the torso and stretched it on his own fingers to re-align the configuration of the victim's prints. A check with Scotland Yard records soon came up with an identity. The remains were those of Stanley Setty, a car dealer who had been reported missing to the Metropolitan Police on Tuesday 4 October. Fortunately for the police, Setty had a record.

Stanely Setty was born Sulman Seti in 1903, in Baghdad, Iraq, of Jewish parents, but the family, penniless, moved to this country when he was just 5 years old. However, by

The torso, where it was discovered on the marshes.

the late 1940s Setty was a wealthy businessman, having risen from petty criminal and black marketeer in the East End to selling cars. He also became involved in various illegal activities, such as acquiring and selling stolen cars, and forging petrol coupons. Single, he lived in a flat in Maitland Court, Lancaster Gate and ran his car business from a garage in Cambridge Terrace Mews, Regents Park, London.

When he was last seen, Setty had just sold a new Wolseley Twelve saloon car to a dealer for £1,000. The buyer paid with a cheque, which later that day was cashed at a bank for 200 £5 notes.

It wasn't long after his disappearance that various people were looking for him, including his sister and brother-in-law, who reported him missing and offered a reward of £1,000 for information as to his whereabouts. However, because of his lifestyle and criminal associates, police were of the opinion that he had been murdered, but there was no trace of a body.

Enquiries quickly led back to Setty's business associate, Brian Donald Fitgerald Hume.

Hume was born out of wedlock in Swanage, Dorset in 1919. Abandoned by his mother, a school teacher, he found himself in the West Country Orphanage, which had a reputation as a particularly brutal institution. It was run by three elderly ladies who showed no love to the children in their care. They even kept a parrot which had been trained to squawk the word 'bastard' every time a child walked by, continually reminding them of their shameful origins. The children were kept short of food, the bedding was thin and filthy, and anyone who stepped out of line would be locked in the pitch-black cellar.

Donald Hume wearing the RAF uniform of an officer.

To enforce discipline, the children were threatened by a visit from the Old Green Gipsy. On occasions, one of the three would dress up as this figure of dread and sneak into the dormitories to terrorise the children at night. Seven-year-old Donald's terror turned to rage one day when he spotted, beneath the green cloak, the shoes of one of his three tormentors. He chased the old woman from the room with an axe.

Eventually, he was removed from the orphanage by his grandmother, but then taken to live with his Aunt Doodie, the headmistress of a Hampshire village school. However, Donald found no love. He was treated as second class, forced to eat separately from the other children, and when Aunt Doodie, her husband and children went on holiday, Donald was left alone. Hume was later to find out that Aunt Doodie was in fact his mother.

At 15 he ran away, hitching his way to London, living off petty crime and seeking somewhere to fit in. At first he was drawn to the Communist Party and the running street fights which were a feature of the 1930s, with Mosley's Blackshirts. At the outbreak of the Second World War he joined the RAF, where he was taught to fly, but he was invalided out in 1941 after suffering from meningitis. The war, however, offered opportunity for Hume and he made a living selling bootleg booze to West End clubs, and dealing in stolen goods. Buying an RAF uniform, he passed himself off as pilot officer Dan Hume, and to add a touch of glamour he awarded himself the DFM.

By the end of the war Hume had married, a child was on the way and he had started a legitimate business, an electrical shop on the Finchley Road. But he could not settle down; he was restless, jealous, ambitious, and, as he was later to write, 'born with a chip on my shoulder against the world'. He wanted quick, easy money. His relationship with

Stanley Setty promised that. Hume was taken in by Setty's wealthy lifestyle and apparently unlimited access to money; something that he was striving to attain himself.

Hume began to lead a double life. On one side he had the legitimate electrical business, and, on the other, he was working for Setty forging petrol coupons and stealing suitable cars to match logbooks that Setty possessed from wrecked cars. The substituted cars would then be re-sprayed, touched up and sold on to unsuspecting customers.

Hume had one other attribute Setty could use, the ability to fly a plane. Smuggling anything from contraband to illegal aliens supported a flourishing black market and Hume became known as the 'Flying Smuggler'.

Scotland Yard had recovered a notebook belonging to Setty which detailed all of his business associates, and they issued the numbers of the £5 notes Setty had obtained from the bank on the morning of his death. Enquiries showed that some of this money had been deposited by Hume into his own bank account. A taxi driver came forward who had been given a £5 with one of the published serial numbers. He told the police that he had driven a customer from Southend Airport to Finchley Road.

Checks were made at airfields in the area and it did not take long before the police discovered that Hume had hired a plane. The net was closing in on Donald Hume.

They knocked on Hume's door at 7.30 a.m. on Thursday, 27 October 1949, and he was taken to Albany Street police station, where he was interviewed by Chief Inspector Jamieson and Superintendent Colin MacDougall. A detailed search of his home in Finchley Road revealed bloodstains under the floorboards. During the interview, Hume kept up a convincing story that he had nothing to do with the murder, but the detectives were one step ahead of him, and confronted with the evidence Hume realised that petty lies were not going to get him off the hook. He then concocted an elaborate story about how he had been offered £150 by three shady smugglers who he only knew as Mac, Greeny and The Boy. He suggested the men must have murdered Setty in his flat to explain away the bloodstains. The men had asked him to drop off some parcels by plane into the sea.

Hume made out that he was desperate for the money and only later realised that the situation was very suspect. Despite his convincing act, the officers did not believe him, and he was charged with the murder of Stanley Setty. His reply to the charge was, 'I am absolutely not guilty.' He appeared at Bow Street Magistrates Court on 29 October and was remanded in custody.

An inquest was opened at Chelmsford on 7 November, when formal identification of the deceased was given by Superintendent Totterdell. Dr Camps told the inquest that death had been caused by stab wounds to the chest, and that after death fractures to the ribs and pelvis had occurred.

On 18 January 1950, Hume appeared before Mr Justice Sellers at the Old Bailey. Sticking to his story that he had not seen Setty on the day of his murder, he also maintained that the bloodstains under the floorboards had come about because the parcels had been in his flat.

The prosecution was led by Mr Christmas Humphries KC, while Hume's defence team was led by Mr R.F. Levey KC. The defence produced a witness who admitted that he had worked in Paris with a gang of car smugglers. He described some of the associates he worked with and some of the names seemed to confirm Hume's story. Was Hume telling the truth about the three men? Had Hume been an unwilling accomplice? It would be left to the jury to decide.

The judge addressed the jury and laid out the various facts and assumptions they had to make. Could Hume's story about the three men delivering parcels containing Setty's body parts be true? Hume had claimed that one of the men pointed a gun at him, but why, asked the judge, would these men trust someone they had only met a few days before? Finally, he reminded the jury that if there was any doubt in the jurors' minds about what happened then they were compelled to return a verdict of not guilty.

The jury retired at noon on 20 January 1950. It took less than three hours for an astonishing verdict to be announced; that they could not agree on a verdict. The foreman of the jury told a hushed court, 'I feel doubtful that we shall reach a unanimous decision.' Setty had escaped the noose. After twelve more jury members were sworn in, the judge directed them to formally return a not guilty verdict to the murder charge. The other indictment which Hume faced – being an accessory after the fact to murder was put to him. Asked if pleaded 'guilty' or 'not guilty' he replied, 'Guilty.' He was sent to twelve years' imprisonment.

Donald Hume was released from Dartmoor Prison on 1 February 1958, having served two-thirds of his sentence. Having been incarcerated and now separated from his wife and child, Hume held a grievance against society. Prison life had not vanquished the chip on his shoulder and as soon as he came out newspaper editors vied for his 'story'.

The *Sunday Pictorial*, a popular tabloid newspaper of the day, approached Hume and offered him £2,000 for his story, a significant sum of money in the late 1950s. Protected by the since-repealed rule of 'double jeopardy', which prevented a person being tried twice for the same crime, he confessed to the murder of Setty. *Sunday Pictorial* readers were fascinated by a front page splash that opened with the words, 'I, Donald Hume, do hereby confess . . . ' In a lurid confession, Hume confessed that he had killed Stanley Setty, cutting up his body and disposing of the remains over the Essex marshes.

The plane used by the Hume to dispose of the body of the Essex marshes.

Changing his name to Donald Brown and with a bogus passport, he took the cash and flew to Zurich to start a new life. But he could not give up his criminal past. As well as attempting to impress a new girlfriend with expensive presents and tales of his life as an American spy, Hume turned to robbing banks when the money ran out. Returning to the UK, he entered the Midland Bank on Boston Manor Road on 1 August 1958, and, walking straight up to cashier Frank Lewis, he shot the bank employee in the stomach before making off with £2,000. Fortunately, Lewis was to survive his injuries. Hume escaped to Kew Bridge station and within twenty-six hours was back with his unsuspecting girlfriend in Zurich.

In January 1959, again desperate for money, he decided to rob the Gewerbe Bank, a bank he was already familiar with. Carrying a cardboard box with a gun hidden inside, Hume entered the bank and, marching straight up to one of the counters, he aimed the gun at cashier Walter Schenkel and fired, before jumping over the counter and rifling the tills. Schenkel was only wounded and managed to set off the alarm bells. Hume ran from the bank pursued by passers-by. Cornered, he turned and fired at the pursuing crowd, which included Arthur Maag, a 50-year-old taxi driver who tried to stop him. Hume shot and killed the brave man, but shortly afterwards he was overpowered and taken into custody.

As there is no capital punishment in Switzerland, Hume was sentenced to life imprisonment with hard labour. However, in 1976, the Swiss authorities re-examined his case. Hume, now 57, thoroughly institutionalised and according to the psychiatrists insane, was repatriated to England, where he was assessed by psychiatrists at Broadmoor Hospital, who confirmed the diagnosis. Hume was to spend the next fifteen years in the hospital before finally being set free in 1991, a confused man of 72.

The story of Donald Hume may have ended there, but there was to be one more twist in the tail. On 19 July 1998, the *Sunday Mirror* reported the following:

A mystery corpse which baffled police for a week has been identified as the body of notorious double-killer Donald Hume. The body was found in the grounds of the Copper Beeches Hotel in Basingstoke, Hampshire, last week, with no clue to the man's identity. But fingerprint checks with Broadmoor revealed it was Hume, once one of the world's most dangerous and deranged post-war murderers. Hume, 78, had been a patient at Broadmoor between 1976 and 1988, before moving to St Bernard's hospital in Southall, Middlesex. A police source said: 'There is no evidence of any foul play in connection with the death and we believe it was probably as a result of natural causes.'

Eleven

THE MURDERED
CHIEF CONSTABLE

Everyone knew who killed William Campling; in fact the person responsible had been arrested for the crime shortly afterwards. The problem was there were no witnesses to the event. William Campling, the Chief Constable of Saffron Walden Borough, had been shot on his own doorstep on Wednesday, 31 October 1849. He received between forty and sixty shotgun pellets in his left leg and more than sixty into his right leg, and lingered in pain before dying from his injuries nine days later.

Saffron Walden lies in the north-west corner of Essex and had had its own police force since 1835, comprising a Chief Constable assisted by two constables. In addition there was a Parish Beadle, who, in 1849, was one James Dewberry. Special Constables would be appointed as and when required on special occasions, such as fairs, when they would receive payment of 1s for carrying out their duties.

Campling had been appointed to the post of Chief Constable in 1848. In July 1849, he had been knocked down in a disturbance when he tried to prevent the 'masses of the lowest order,' from entering a show being presented by a company of strolling players on the common.

The man accused of the murder was 21-year-old Benjamin Pettit, with whom Campling had previously had dealings with and who was known to bear a grudge against the Chief Constable.

When it became apparent that Campling would not recover from his injuries, the Mayor, Nathaniel Catlin, decided to take a deposition from him, in the presence of Pettit. Campling stated:

On the 31st day of October last, about ten minutes past ten in the evening, I left the Eight Bells public house in Bridge Street, which is about forty yards from my house, but on the opposite side of the way. When I came out of the Eight Bells, I saw William Brand of

James Dewberry, the Parish Beadle for Saffron Walden, who assisted in the arrest of Benjamin Pettit.

The Eight Bells public house. Campling had left the premises just prior to his murder.

North End, Bailiff for Mr Martin Nockolds. We entered into conversation for a minute or two and he walked as far as my door with me. I was in the act of opening my door. I bid him good night, and immediately he left me I was shot in my legs, which drove me into my door ...After I got upstairs I told them to go and see where Pettit was, or where he had been... My reason for saying so was because he had threatened me at other times, the last time... was when I met him in the passage down by the Abbey Lane Chapel... three or four months ago. I met him on a sudden, I think his expression was in sort of wrath:'You old—, you—; I'll do your business for you one of these times.'

On Friday, 9 November 1849, a jury was empanelled before W.E. Freeland, coroner for the Borough of Saffron Walden. A number of witnesses were called to give evidence at the inquest. Surgeon Thomas Brown and his assistant, Mr Dickenson, had attended within a few minutes of the attack and found Campling hysterical. They carried him upstairs. The next morning they extracted eight shots from the right leg and two from the left leg. Brown then found jaundice showing and the next day, gangrene. Dr Paget, of Cambridge, also attended but the situation was hopeless and they later agreed that death was solely attributable to the effects of the shooting. Questioned by a member of the jury, the surgeon said that amputation would have caused his immediate death from shock.

The Borough Watch Committee turned for help to the Essex Constabulary in an effort to find evidence to convict Pettit of the crime, but this proved fruitless and they next turned to the Metropolitan Police, who sent Inspector Lund to Saffron Walden to look into the case. He also failed to find any evidence to connect Pettit to the crime, although he did manage to put in a claim for expenses which amounted to some £15, and which included a claim for 12s 6d for 'knifes and braces'.

The Watch Committee once again turned for help from the Essex Constabulary, but Superintendent Clark from Newport, who was in charge of policing for the surrounding area, and the Chief Constable, Captain (later Admiral) John McHardy refused to intervene further in the matter.

Depositions were taken from twenty-one witnesses, including Mary Brewer, the daughter of a pork butcher who lived in the house adjoining the Camplings' house in Bridge Street, who told the inquest that she was at home about 10 p.m., when stones were thrown at the door. Soon after, she was upstairs with Miss Campling when they saw Mr Campling coming home. They heard a shot fired from the opposite side of the road and went downstairs to find him lying in the street by the front door. William Brand, who had walked with Campling to his door, then began walking up Windmill Hill Road towards North End when he heard a loud bang and saw smoke coming from the direction of Francis Gibson's garden wall, and then heard the officer say, 'I'm shot! I'm shot!'

Witness after witness gave evidence to the inquest. Pettit, the jury were told, had spent the day of the shooting in the Waggon and Horses public house in Castle Street until about eleven in the evening, except he was missing for an hour or so from nine o'clock. During that missing hour he had taken two guns belonging to the landlord of the Waggon and Horses, Thomas Porter.

John Brewer, 15, also heard the shot and saw Campling lying by his door. He noticed a white dog – 'rough headed with a short tail' – near the spot from where the fatal shot had been fired. This dog had often been seen in Pettit's company when he had been engaged in ratting, although Pettit was to claim that the dog actually belonged to Porter.

The jury reassembled on Monday the 12th to examine the evidence of Thomas Porter of the Waggon and Horses. Porter admitted to owning the two guns, which he had let Pettit use only when he was present. One was single-barrelled calibre about the size of a sixpenny piece. Mary and Sarah Porter, his wife and daughter, were examined, but the two women, like Porter, gave evidence in such an unsatisfactory manner that the coroner and jury gave up the attempt to elicit anything useful from them.

The jury again reconvened on the 14th, when Mr Paine, clerk to solicitor Thurgood, said that he and the Excise Officer, Mr Bedwell, were in King's Street late on the evening in question when they saw Pettit walking towards Almshouse Lane, with his hands in his pockets, whistling, and accompanied by a white dog. They spoke to Pettit until the arrival of a constable, who arrested him and conveyed him to the Mayor's house, where several of the Magistrates were gathered. On their way to the house Pettit made an attempt to escape his captors, but was unsuccessful.

In spite of the evidence presented to the inquest, the coroner's jury were unable to say that Pettit was responsible for the murder and returned a verdict that:

> Some person unknown, not having the fear of God before his eyes, but moved and seduced by the instigation of the devil... with force of arms... did make an assault upon the said William Campling and the said person unknown a certain gun charged and loaded with gunpowder and leaden shot which he did fire at the legs of William Campling and gave several wounds of which he languished and on the ninth day of November did.

Pettit, however, was not in the clear. He had already been charged with 'Shooting with intent' and was remanded in custody at Springfield Gaol, to await his trial at the next Assize court.

Benjamin Pettit, having been in custody since November, appeared before the judge at the Essex Lent Assize, held at Shire Hall in the second week of March 1850. Prosecution counsel Russell Gurney QC laid out the facts and identified three inferences that could be made; first that the shooting had not been an accident, for the stones thrown against the door were intended to get Campling to a place where he could be shot; secondly that it was certain that the crime was not for plunder but was the result of ill-feeling towards the victim; and thirdly that the assailant had concealed himself near the bridge over a small stream to commit the crime. Much of the evidence given at the inquest was repeated; William Payne, clerk to the magistrates, spoke of the deposition Campling made before his death, with the prisoner present.

Memorial to William Campling, erected near the spot where he was murdered.

Superintendent Clarke and Inspector Lunn from the Detective Service of the Metropolitan Police both gave evidence about the footprints found near the scene of the shooting. Henry Shuttleworth, ironmonger, examined the shot taken by Constable Wright from Pettit's home. He found them to be size 3, 4 and 5 (mixed), exactly matching the three types removed by Browne from the dying Campling. That was the case for the prosecution.

Mr T. Chambers led for the defence and addressed the jury. His argument was that all the evidence presented to the court was circumstantial. He said that the whole town was against Pettit and that a month had been spent not seeking to apprehend the real killer, but in proving the guilt of his client. After the judge had summed up, the jury retired to consider their verdict. A quarter of an hour later they returned to the court with a verdict of 'Not Guilty'.

A subsequent entry in Corporation Accounts for 1850 showed that £15 was paid by way of compensation to Campling's family.

Following Campling's death, the Watch Committee appointed James Goss as his replacement in March 1852, but he lasted only four months. Sergeant Benjamin Rudd was appointed Chief Constable in July 1852. His salary was fixed at 25s per week, and he was allowed to occupy the police cottage at the back of the Town Hall in Butcher Row. Judd resigned in 1856 and a circular was sent out to various authorities advertising the vacancy: 'Cash salary sixty-five pounds. Residence free, a new suit and two pairs of boots, a new cape and Great Coat every two years.'

Eventually, on 1 November 1857, the force was amalgamated with the Essex Constabulary. Superintendent Clark posted an inspector and four constables to police the town.

Twelve

WARTIME MURDERS

Crime and particularly murder increased dramatically in England and Wales during the Second World War, rising from 115 in 1940 to 141 in 1945, an increase of 22 per cent. Execution did not automatically follow conviction of murder and in most years eight out of ten murders were not followed by execution. In Essex, soldiers were responsible for six deaths, and in only one case was a conviction for murder not given. Three took place in 1943, two in 1944 and one at the end of the war in 1945. In three of the cases those found guilty paid the ultimate price for their crime.

'I did not realise what I was doing until it was too late'

Private William Henry Turner was just 19 years old when he appeared before the Essex Assizes in January 1943, charged with the murder of 82-year-old widow Ann Elizabeth Wade at her home in Audley Road, Colchester. A native of Doncaster, Turner went absent without leave from his unit, and, purporting to be a corporal on leave and unable to find accommodation, he called at Mrs Wade's house, asked for a cup of tea and was offered a job digging her garden. When it began to rain, the elderly widow invited him into her home, where he repaid her kindness by strangling her with the scarf she was wearing. He hid the body under the bed, stole some money and left, but was soon apprehended and charged with murder.

The jury failed to reach a verdict on the charge of murder and Mr Justice Asquith discharged them and ordered a new jury to hear the case. This time he was convicted, but with a recommendation from the jury for mercy. However their plea fell on deaf ears and he was sentenced to death. Turner appealed to the Court of Criminal Appeal against his conviction on the grounds that the judge had misdirected the jury in failing to distinguish between murder and manslaughter. However his appeal was refused and he was executed on Wednesday 24 March at Pentonville Prison.

The Rayleigh Bath Chair Murder

About 2 p.m. on 23 July 1943, the residents of Hockley Road, Rayleigh were startled by the sound of an explosion. Although not unusual during wartime, there had been no prior warning of enemy action. Near a house called 'Gattens', a short distance from Rayleigh town centre, residents were confronted by a scene of carnage. There was a devastating tangle of metal and human remains in the road. The left leg of a victim was hanging 15ft high in a nearby tree; the right was found 48ft away in a front garden. It was obvious that there was nothing that could be done for the person concerned. A woman lay screaming in the road nearby.

Experts were called and quickly discounted the possibility of a bomb, and from pieces recovered from the scene police ascertained that the detonation had been caused by an anti-tank mine known as the No. 75 Hawkins Grenade. The wreckage was found to be that of a bath chair and the woman identified as Mrs Doris Irene Mitchell who, it turned out, was a private nurse employed to look after 47-year-old invalid Archibald Brown of London Hill, Rayleigh. Brown came from a family that had long owned Rayleigh Mill, trading as T.J. Brown & Son. Nurse Mitchell told the police that the man who had been sitting in the bath chair was indeed Archibald Brown.

Hockley Road, showing the spot where the explosion took place.

The remains of the bath chair after the explosion.

Assistant Chief Constable John Crockford, who recalled Superintendent Totterdell from leave to investigate the death of Archibald Brown.

Superintendent George Totterdell, who was in charge of the CID in Essex, was recalled from leave by the Assistant Chief Constable, John Crockford, to lead the investigation into Brown's untimely death.

The story that emerged was that Archibald Brown, after three years service as a soldier of the Great War, had become a successful miller. However he had been severely injured in a motorcycle accident at the age of 24, and twenty-three years later he was crippled, pain-ridden and unable to walk. His willpower, however, was undiminished and he ruled his family with a rod of iron. His wife was not even allowed to visit her mother in nearby Rochford. One example of his embittered character was the bell that he rang constantly to get his wife's attention. His elder son, Eric, who was 19 years old, was constantly beaten and humiliated, but by 1943 their relationship appeared to be on a more even keel. Totterdell discovered that Eric was serving as a Private in the Suffolk Regiment, but was currently at home on compassionate leave. Interestingly, Todderdell discovered that he had been trained in the use of the Hawkins Grenade, which was designed for use by infantrymen to blow the tracks from tanks.

Had the mine been fitted under the seat of the bath chair? How had it been detonated? Why had it not gone off previously? These were all questions which vexed Totterdell. Nurse Mitchell was interviewed when she had recovered from her injuries. Amazingly, as she was only a few feet from the explosion, she escaped with only minor injuries. Archibald Brown had taken the full force of the explosion, but the frame and cushions of the bath chair had shielded her.

Nurse Mitchell told the detective that the chair was normally kept in the air-raid shelter at the London Hill home, and at 1.45 p.m. on 23 July she had gone to get it. She had found the shelter door locked from the inside, and, returning with Mrs Brown, had met Eric coming out. He was irritated and evasive. Both women then wheeled the chair to the house then helped Archibald to get in. He was wearing pyjamas and a dressing gown and they covered him with a plaid travelling rug. Finally they adjusted two pillows and a blanket around him, tucking the rug under the cushion of his chair. One mile down the Hockley Road the patient wanted a cigarette and fumbled in his dressing gown pocket. The nurse went to the front of the chair to light his cigarette, after which she went back behind the chair and pushed him forward. Within half a dozen paces there was a tremendous explosion.

Doris Brown, in the course of a five-hour interview at Rayleigh police station, stated that her husband had increasingly appeared to take a dislike to her. Eric too had noticed the deterioration in Archibald's behaviour. His father had liked his new nurse and enjoyed their walks together, although there was no suggestion of any impropriety or jealousy. Doris had considered her son Eric to be mechanically minded; he was capable of repairing their radio. Eric himself suffered mood swings and the relationship with his family was such that he had been moved from his school at Rayleigh to a boarding school near Walthamstow. Between 1940 and 1942 he had worked at Barclays Bank in Rochford, until a period of bizarre behaviour had caused the manager to seek his resignation. On 1 October 1942 he was called up for the army and posted to Spilsby in Lincolnshire. In his camp was a store of about 200 Hawkins Grenades, at least 144 of which were operational. The explosive device was about 7in by 4in and looked rather like a large cycle lamp.

Before Eric Brown was interviewed, the police held a conference at Headquarters. Tests were carried out on similar chairs. It was decided that it was reasonable to assume that a pressure plate had been adapted to lessen the weight required to explode the mine. There was considerable difference between pressure from a tank and that of a human body.

The young soldier was interviewed by Totterdell, in the presence of Detective Chief Inspector Draper and Detective Inspector Jack 'Trapper' Barkway. The latter then wrote down Brown's confession, which asserted that his mother had been made a drudge and was living a completely intolerable life. 'I decided that the only real way in which my mother could lead a normal life and my father to be released from his sufferings was for him to die mercifully.' He said that he had brought the grenade home from the army and put it under his father's seat, having adjusted the top plate. He was arrested and charged with murder.

Appearing at Southend County Petty Sessions on 21 September 1943, he was committed for trial at the next Essex Assizes. On 4 November he appeared before Mr Justice Atkinson at Chelmsford and pleaded 'not guilty'. Most of the facts were undisputed, although a suggestion was made to Detective Inspector Barkway that Chief Inspector Draper had intimated that 'if Brown did not confess, things could be worse for his mother.' This was strenuously denied. But the prisoner's main defence rested on the question of his sanity. Barkway gave evidence of previous family background and behaviour. One defence doctor diagnosed Eric as schizophrenic. The doctor who examined the prisoner gave his opinion that Brown was sane, but reported that, whilst in custody, he had attempted to cut his own throat. The jury found him 'guilty but insane' and he was sentenced to be detained during His Majesty's pleasure.

Totterdell's autobiography was published by Harrap in 1956 with the title *Country Copper*. His supposition was that Archibald Brown shifted his weight after the nurse had lit his cigarette and that Eric Brown, having altered the pressure plate on the device, caused it to explode. His conclusion was that the question remained – and still remains – why the explosion did not occur when the victim was first lowered onto the chair? Perhaps that was what Eric intended, but at that location he might also have killed his mother as well as his father and the nurse. There was no apparent financial reason for his action and he must have known that he would be a prime suspect. Did he not consider the possibility of the death or serious injury of Nurse Mitchell? He must also have been certain of their route. Had the nurse chosen to make a right turn into the High Street there could have been many more casualties.

Nurse Mitchell recovered but was left with a limp and permanent injury to her arm. Eric Brown was finally released in 1975 after spending thirty-two years in an asylum.

The Birch Taxi Cab Murder

Foul play was suspected when a Vauxhall taxi cab was found abandoned by a patrolling constable, PC 505 McCormack, in Haynes Green Lane, Layer Marney, on 8 December 1943.

A bloodstained jacket and raincoat were found in the vehicle, but there was no sign of the driver, Henry Claude Hailstone. Detective Superintendent George Totterdell, assisted by Detective Inspector Draper, were assigned to the case. When the two detectives made enquiries at his lodgings in Maldon Road, Colchester, his landlady, Mrs Pearce, identified the clothing as belonging to her lodger. She told police she'd last seen the 28 year old at ten past eleven on the night of 7 December. A taxi driver by trade, Hailstone had called in to tell her he would be late in for his supper, as he had to take two American servicemen to their camp at Birch. He added that he expected to be back in about half an hour, but when he failed to return his landlady thought he must have run out of petrol, which at the time was strictly rationed, and had decided to sleep in his cab.

A search of the taxi's bloodstained interior showed signs of a struggle, the driver overpowered and dumped on the back seat, his cab then being driven to where it was found abandoned. An empty wallet was found on the floor of the car. But where was Hailstone? Totterdell concluded that Hailstone must have been attacked by someone sitting in the rear of the cab, his assailant then driving it to where it was found abandoned. A search of the immediate area revealed no signs of a body.

The next day the search was widened, concentrating on the roads leading to the five American bases in the Birch area. Eventually his battered body was discovered in the grounds of Birch Rectory. A post-mortem was carried out by Dr Camps, who found death had been caused by manual strangulation. There was bruising on the face from at least three heavy blows, and marks on the neck indicated that they had been made by somebody with a strong left hand. Hailstone was well built and weighed 12 stone, and police believed that it may have taken more than one person to carry his body to where it was found.

Inquiries narrowed the search for his killers down to two black American privates, George E. Fowler, E Company, 356th Engineers Regiment, and J.C. Leatherberry.

The body of Henry Hailstone, where it was discovered in the grounds of Birch Rectory.

Photograph of Private George Fowler taken after his arrest.

Photograph of Private J. Leatherberry taken after his arrest.

Interviewed by Totterdell, Fowler denied all knowledge of the crime. He said that on 7 December he had been on a pub crawl in London. He couldn't remember how he had got back to camp, but when he woke up he was wearing a sergeant's shirt. He had no idea how he had got hold of it. A search of the hut where he slept discovered a soldier's shirt bearing sergeant's stripes, with what appeared to be traces of blood on it.

Interviewed again, Fowler said that he had gone to London where he had met Private J.C. Leatherberry of A Company, 356th Engineers Regiment. Fowler told the investigators that on arriving at Colchester they had decided to hire a taxi and rob the driver. At 10.45 p.m. they had flagged down a cab, and had covered four miles on their way to Birch when he asked the driver to stop so that he could get out to relieve himself. While he was out of the taxi, Leatherberry, who had remained in the cab, called out to him. He saw Leatherberry standing on the floor of the back of the cab, holding the driver in the front seat with his left hand and punching him in the face. The driver went limp and Leatherberry hauled Hailstone into the back of the cab. Fowler claimed that he had gone along with the escapade unwillingly. Leatherberry had told him, 'We're in this together, man. And now we've got to get rid of him.' They had dumped the driver's body, but not before they had rifled his pockets.

Henry Hailstone.

On 13 December, Totterdell interviewed Leatherberry, who denied any involvement. A search of his hut revealed a bloodstained shirt, pants and vest. On 19 December both men were handed over into the custody of the Commanding Officer of the 356th Engineering Regiment. Both men were charged with murder and robbery and appeared before a General Court Martial at the Town Hall in Ipswich on Wednesday, 19 January 1944. Fowler was tried first and attempted to place the blame on Leatherberry. However, he was found guilty and sentenced to life imprisonment. Leatherberry was also found guilty and sentenced to death, and was hanged at Shepton Mallet military prison on 16 May 1944.

An American serviceman, Lawson France, was involved in another case in May 1944, which resulted in the death of Percy James Knock at Birch, near Colchester. Reporting back to his camp, France told his senior officer that he had been involved in a fight in a nearby field with a civilian. A search discovered the body of Knock, who had been strangled. The two men had met in a local public house, and when France left, Knock followed him; a conversation took place between them and they went to a field, where a sexual act took place. Afterwards there was a fight, during which Knock was strangled. At a subsequent court martial France was found not guilty of murder.

'It's a case of killing, my name is Private Jones'

Totterdell was called in to investigate another case of murder involving a soldier in June 1944. On the evening of Thursday 22 June, Edgar Lilley was at his home in Colchester when there was a loud knocking on his front door. Upon opening the door, he discovered a young soldier wearing the uniform of the Somerset Light Infantry. He appeared agitated and asked Lilley to call the police. When Detective Constable Hart arrived at the house, the soldier told the startled officer: 'It's a case of killing, my name is Private Jones'. The previous night he had stolen 15s from the barrack room while the remainder of his platoon had been out training. Afraid to face his comrades when they returned, he had absconded, taking a sten-gun and ammunition with him. He said he intended to rob a civilian and take his clothes. He had walked onto the marshes, and, while crossing fields, had come across an officer who was carrying a shotgun.

Jones said that the officer had questioned him and, not satisfied with the answer he had given, told him to hand over the sten-gun. He refused and the two men struggled. 'I lost my head and shot him. I must have been mad. I threw the sten-gun away. All this happened about three hours ago. I will take you there.' Jones then led the detective to Abberton and, walking across a field, he pointed to a hedge in the corner and said, 'The officer's in there.' Jones was then taken to the police station in Abberton and detained.

Totterdell was informed and at first light the next morning a pathologist made a preliminary examination. Death, in his opinion, was due to a series of bullet wounds in the upper part of the body. A local officer at the scene recognised the dead man as Captain Samuel Herbert Grundy, a 57-year-old regular Army officer, currently attached to the 18th Battalion Essex Home Guard. The body was formally identified by the unit Company Sergeant-Major J.H. Blount, who said that he had last seen Captain Grundy at 7.15 p.m. when he had left the Battalion Headquarters, based at Bull Farm, with the intention of shooting rabbits.

Interviewed by Totterdell and Detective Chief Inspector Draper, Jones made a detailed statement. He told the officers that he had met Grundy on the marshes, who asked him what he was doing and asked him to hand over the sten-gun he was carrying. There was a struggle and Jones shot Grundy. He said, 'I thought he was dead. He ought to have been.' He threw the sten-gun away.

A post-mortem revealed that Grundy had been shot six times in the upper body.

Jones appeared before Mr Justice Singleton at the Essex assize on 8 November 1944, charged with murder. His defence counsel, addressing the jury, stressed the alternative verdict of manslaughter on the grounds of the accused's temper becoming so inflamed as to become ungovernable. If in the heat of violent struggle or quarrel a person took a human life, that act might not be murder but manslaughter. Furthermore, there was the point that any attempt to take a weapon from an armed soldier was a hazardous thing to do.

The jury took only twenty minutes to reach a verdict – manslaughter. The court was told of Jones' previous history. The product of a broken home, he had spent several periods in Borstal and on his release in February 1944 he had enlisted in the Army. Mr Justice Singleton, in sentencing Jones, said, 'I cannot imagine a worse case of manslaughter.' He was sentenced to penal servitude for fifteen years.

'I had not the smallest intention of killing anyone'

James McNicoll was born in Motherwell, Scotland in 1918 of working class parents. At the outbreak of the Second World War James joined up and served with some distinction in the Royal Artillery. By 1944 he had reached the rank of sergeant. He fought for his king and country in Africa and the Middle East but whilst in Africa he contracted malaria. He had something of a temper and was known to the police. By early 1945 McNicoll was serving at a heavy anti-aircraft battery, at Thorpe Bay near Southend, and shared a Nissen hut with fellow sergeants Leonard Cox and Donald Kirkaldie. He and 26-year-old Don Kirkaldie became firm friends.

On 16 August that year, a dance was being held in the NAAFI to celebrate VE-Day (the war ended on the 15th with the surrender of Japan), and McNicoll was annoyed to see his girlfriend, Jean Neale, dancing with airman Jerald McKay and there was an altercation between the two men. Kirkaldie and Cox tried to calm the situation, but McNicoll, who had been drinking heavily, threatened to fight Cox.

In the early hours, when Kirkaldie and Cox were asleep in the Nissen hut, they were suddenly awoken when one of the hut's windows was broken. They saw a hand come in through the broken pane and the light was switched on. Seconds later the muzzle of a rifle appeared and a shot rang out, wounding Cox. A second shot hit Kirkaldie in the throat, killing him instantly. McNicoll was soon identified as the guilty party and was arrested by the police.

According to his statement, McNicoll said, 'I had no intentions of killing Cox but I wanted to wound him.' He told the police that he had gone back to the sergeant's hut, broken the window and switched the light on. He then tried to shoot Sergeant Cox in the leg. He fired another shot and then in a dazed state, knowing he had done something seriously wrong, ran away. At this stage he was completely unaware that he had killed his best mate, Sergeant Kirkaldie. A little later he found himself in a field and decided to bury the rifle. He fell asleep fully clothed and remained there until he was woken by the police later on that morning. James offered no resistance when he was arrested and co-operated fully with the police, giving an open and truthful statement. When he was charged with murder, he told the police immediately where he had buried the rifle. It was found in a field behind the Coastguard Station at Thorpe Bay.

The trial opened at the Essex Assizes in Chelmsford before Mr Justice Lewis on 13 November 1945 and lasted two days. The jury comprised ten men and two women. Mr Cecil Havers KC appeared for the prosecution while Mr Tristram Beresford KC defended the accused. McNicoll was charged with murder and attempted murder. He pleaded not guilty to both charges. In the witness box he asserted that he had never intended to kill Sergeant Kirkaldie and explained that when he went back to the sergeant's hut to go to bed, he found the door locked and became angry. He told the court that this is what made him break the window and fire a shot. He then stepped back and fired a second shot generally at the hut. 'Having got so far I fired the rifle twice'. He told the court that he didn't aim but just fired wildly, 'I had not the smallest intention of killing anyone. I only wanted to frighten Cox. I was dazed. I knew I had done wrong. I ran away from the camp and buried the rifle.'

Mr Tristram Beresford invited the jury to bring in a verdict of manslaughter on the grounds that James was too drunk to form any intention of killing anyone, but this was rejected by the jury. In his summing up, Mr Justice Lewis told the jury that although during the trial there had been references to James' jealousy over Jean Neale, there was no suggestion that McNicoll had any cause to be jealous insofar as Sergeant Kirkaldie was concerned.

The jury retired to consider their verdict and soon returned and declared James guilty on both charges. Mr Justice Lewis then donned the black cap and sentenced James 'to be taken back to the prison where he was last confined and from there to a place of execution, there to be hanged by the neck until dead and that thereafter his body be buried in the precincts of the prison.' He added the customary rider, 'May the Lord have mercy upon your soul.' James was taken down from the dock and transferred back to prison.

McNicoll appealed against his conviction and this was heard on Wednesday 5 December by the Court of Appeal. The defence submission was that James was under the influence of drink so as to be incapable of forming any intention to murder. However, in his judgement, Lord Justice Humphreys, one of the three Lord Justices of Appeal in Ordinary, accepted that everyone agreed that James was so drunk as to make himself a nuisance and his own evidence made it clear that he acted as he did because he had a quarrel with another man (Sergeant Cox) who was in the hut. The appeal was dismissed as it was plain from the evidence that James had gone to the hut intending to do someone an injury and a man had died as a result. 'Thank you, my lord,' McNicoll said as he left the dock.

McNicoll was removed to Pentonville Prison, as Chelmsford Prison had ceased to carry out executions in 1914. He was hanged by Albert Pierrepoint at 9.30 a.m. on Friday 21 December. McNicoll's execution was unusual in that it was one of two that day – for completely unrelated crimes. At 8 a.m., John Riley Young was hanged for the murder of Frederick Lucas and his wife Cassie in June 1945. Young had also been tried at Chelmsford and had lost his appeal on the same day as James. After Young's execution his body was left to hang for the usual hour. It was then removed, the trapdoors reset and the gallows prepared for McNicoll.

Thirteen

THE RISE AND FALL
OF ALFRED MARDEN

Police officers need many skills and abilities to do their job effectively. Nowadays, each officer is regularly given specialist advice, which ensures that he or she follows a career pattern best suited to balancing their own ambitions with the needs of the service. Career development advice thus helps officers follow a career path which recognises their particular abilities.

In the nineteenth century, career paths were less sophisticated and it was more difficult to recognise good work or brave conduct. This realisation led to Chief Constable Admiral McHardy introducing the Merit Star in 1871, for 'highly distinguished conduct in the discharge of their duty, particularly when accompanied by a risk to life, personal courage and coolness, aided by marked intelligence.'

Many forces had already introduced a Merit Star, which had long been advocated by Her Majesty's Inspector of Constabulary. Constables were to receive an extra shilling per week in their pay, sergeants two shillings. The badge was to be worn on the collar next to the officer's number (later on the right sleeve) and he could forfeit it through misconduct. A maximum of twenty constables and ten sergeants could hold the Merit Star at any one time, before its use finally fell into decline in the middle of this century.

Alfred John Marden's eventual rise to the rank of superintendent probably owed a lot to the way he reacted to an early incident in his career. Marden was born in 1863 at Writtle, near Chelmsford, the son of a hay binder, and he joined the Essex Constabulary in 1883 at the age of 20. His first post was as a groom at Headquarters, before moving to the Brentwood Division. On Tuesday, 20 January 1885, instead of pounding the beat, he was ordered to patrol the Rainham area in a pony and trap with Inspector Thomas Simmons, from Romford. Simmons was himself the holder of the Merit Star, earned when he was a constable. During their patrol they were told about the activities of three suspicious men seen in the area, and it was not long before they came across them near Blewitts Farm.

Superintendent Alfred Marden, wearing the Merit Star on his collar.

As Marden questioned one of the men, Inspector Simmons spoke to the other two. The man questioned by Marden was David Dredge, a well-known London criminal. He suddenly pulled a revolver out of his pocket, pointed it at Marden and threatened to shoot. Almost immediately a shot rang out and the officer spun round to see Inspector Simmons staggering back and clutching his stomach. Without a thought for his own safety, Marden ran towards Simmons, who was badly wounded, and then gave chase after the men. Contemporary accounts show that Marden was threatened by two of the three men, both of whom fired at him, but he refused to give up the chase, despite receiving further threats. Eventually they were able to give him the slip and he returned to where Inspector Simmons had collapsed, finding him in great pain. He drove the injured officer to Dagenham police station for treatment, but four days after the shooting Simmons died from his injuries.

A huge search was carried out for all three men, led by Superintendent Dobson from Brentwood. Two were subsequently arrested, Dredge and a man called James Lee. Both men were tried at the Central Criminal Court, as the feeling against them in Essex made it too dangerous. Dredge was acquitted of the murder, but was immediately re-arrested for threatening to shoot Marden and eventually received twelve months' hard labour. Lee was found guilty and sentenced to death. The third man, John Martin, part of another gang, was eventually arrested in Cumbria, following the murder of several other policemen, and was eventually hanged for those crimes. Marden was awarded the Merit Star and received his extra shilling a week – a much-deserved award. Simmons received a hero's burial, and an appeal for his widow raised over £1,000; a huge sum in those days.

As a result of this tragedy, Essex police officers who patrolled beats bordering the Metropolitan Police area were allowed to carry revolvers on night duty for their own protection. The presence of armed police officers on our streets is not a modern image, but was reality over 130 years ago.

After Marden's bravery was recognised by the award of the Merit Star, his career path was guaranteed. Within three years he was promoted to the rank of Acting Sergeant and a posting to Southend, where he was promoted to Sergeant in 1891. In 1898 he moved to Clacton, and in 1901 was promoted Inspector at Romford. In 1903 he was again promoted, this time to Superintendent, and put in charge of the Brentwood Division. He retired in 1913 and died at the age of 71 in 1934.

During his long service Marden took part in the investigation of a number of sensational murder cases that occurred in Essex.

The Prittlewell Murder

Sergeant Marden assisted in the investigation into the murder of 18-year-old Florence Dennis, whose body was discovered in Gainsborough Drive, Prittlewell on 24 June 1894. She had been shot in the head. The enquiry, which was conducted jointly by Marden and Detective Inspector Baker of the Metropolitan Police, found that Florence was pregnant, and the mistress of 39-year-old James Canham Read, a married man with eight children, who was employed as a cashier in the Royal Albert Docks in London. Florence had no hesitation in naming Read as the father and wrote to him asking what his intentions towards her were. They agreed to meet in Southend, but when Florence failed to return home from the meeting, her concerned sister (who incidentally had also been a mistress of Read) wrote to him asking him if he knew where her sister was.

Read panicked and stole money from his office and went on the run. Wanted posters were circulated with his description. He was eventually arrested at the home of another of his mistresses in Mitcham, Surrey, and tried at the Essex Assizes. Found guilty, he was hanged at Chelmsford Prison on 4 December 1894.

Because of the skills he showed on the case, Marden was made a Detective Sergeant (Baker was later

Superintendent Samuel Hawtree, who was in charge of the investigation of the murder of Florence Dennis at Southend.

to become Chief Constable of Hastings). When Alfred Marden moved from Southend, the residents presented him with a cheque for £100, a considerable sum in those days, together with an illuminated address which read, 'his courage, tact and discretion have earned words of appreciation from the presiding Justices of the Chief Courts of Essex, and as a most zealous and astute officer he has merited the full confidence of all who have had occasion to appreciate his untiring energies in the cause of law and justice.'

The Moat Farm Murder

In 1901, Marden was promoted to Detective Inspector and moved to Romford. In 1903, he was brought in to enquire into the circumstances surrounding the disappearance of Camille Holland, a 56-year-old spinster, from her home at Moat Farm, Clavering, where she had set up home with Samuel Herbert Dougal.

She had been missing for three years, and stories abounded about Dougal, who was a renowned womaniser in the locality. Called in by the Chief Constable Captain Showers to investigate Dougal's financial affairs, Marden was able to show that Dougal had been forging Miss Holland's signature on cheques from the time of her disappearance in 1899. Dougal was arrested and when Moat Farm was searched the remains of Camille Holland were discovered buried in a drainage ditch. Although the body was badly decomposed, she was identified by the remains of the shoes she was wearing, which had been made for her by a local cobbler.

Moat Farm, Clavering, where Samuel Herbert Dougal and Miss Holland lived as husband and wife.

The body of Camille Holland just after it had been discovered in the drainage ditch at the Moat Farm.

The funeral of Miss Holland at Saffron Walden cemetery.

Dougal was tried for her murder at Chelmsford and hanged at Chelmsford Prison in July 1903.

Miss Holland was buried in the cemetery at Saffron Walden, the funeral being attended by a large number of people.

Marden's conduct in the case earned him an award of £15 from the Standing Joint Committee (Police Committee).

The Warley Gap Murder

In 1903 Marden was placed in charge of the Brentwood Division, but he had hardly settled into his new role when he was called upon to investigate a case which was to become known as the Warley Gap Murder. Private Bernard White, a 21-year-old soldier in the 2nd Battalion Essex Regiment, appeared before Mr Justice Lawrence at the Essex Assizes on 12 November, charged with the wilful murder of Maud Garrett at Little Warley on 22 May 1903. He pleaded not guilty to the offence. Mr Gill KC led for the prosecution and Mr Forrest Fulton for the defence.

The Essex Regiment at the time of the murder were stationed at their barracks at Warley. The deceased was the daughter of Daniel Garrett, a bricklayer from Brentwood, and she was described in court as a respectable girl. She had made the acquaintance of White and the two were on friendly if not affectionate terms until the end of 1901, when White was posted with his Battalion to South Africa to fight in the Boer War, returning to this country in early May 1903. Whilst White was abroad, Maud had become engaged to Private Cecil Jones of the RAMC. By chance White met Maud on the 21st of that month, the day before she was murdered, and he arranged to meet her again on the evening of the 22nd. They were seen by several witnesses together during the evening, but, at 10 p.m., White left Maud to return to his barracks. Soon after, however, he left the barracks and went after Maud. About 10.30 p.m., an officer from the barracks heard screaming coming from an area known as the Warley Gap. White returned to the barracks about 11 p.m. Early the next morning, a labourer on his way to work found the battered body of Maud lying in woodland. She had been beaten around the head with a blunt object, which the doctors who examined the body believed had been caused by a stick or cane. It was known that White often walked out carrying a cane.

White was arrested and interviewed by Marden and admitted to meeting the girl on the 21st and the 22nd, leaving her at the gate to the barracks and not seeing her again, although he said he did go out again to find her. However, he denied any involvement in her death. His belongings were searched and police found traces of blood on his boots, socks, trousers and cane. Marden charged him with the murder but White made no reply.

After Mr Justice Lawrence had summed up, the jury retired to consider their verdict, and returned forty-nine minutes later with a guilty verdict. White was sentenced to death and was hanged by Henry Pierrepoint at Chelmsford Prison on 1 December.

The Basildon Bungalow Murder

In 1906, Marden investigated the double murder of a married couple in Honeypot Lane, Basildon.

In 1906, a reporter from the *Southend Telegraph* described it as 'little more than a track five miles from Billericay, five miles from Pitsea, extending from the main road to the Laindon Road,' whilst the *Essex Weekly News* described the location as 'one of the most inaccessible districts of Essex'. Honeypot Lane still exists to this day, but as a quarter-mile long row of council dwellings stretching along the east side of present-day Gloucester Park.

'Half a mile from the Basildon Rectory,' was one description of the location of the wooden bungalow where Mr and Mrs Watson lived. Albert Watson, aged 47, and his 50-year-old wife Emma were quiet neighbours and churchgoers, having moved from Kilburn. Their smallholding was well stocked and tended – but there was just one problem, they did not have water on their plot and so they obtained it from a pond on the land of their neighbour, Mr Buckham of Sawyers Farm, who lived with his wife and their two sons, Richard, aged 19, and Robert, aged 16. Buckham had a job in London and left each day for work at 6 a.m. Wednesday, 23 August 1906 was no exception.

About 10 o'clock that day Richard and Robert ran to the main Billericay road and told a Mr Stevens that two people had been drowned in the pond. Neighbours were summoned and went to the pond where they saw the body of Albert Watson almost submerged and that of his wife lying close by it. The police were called and the bodies examined – both had been shot, the man twice in the groin and the woman once in the chest. A search of the immediate area failed to find a weapon. When Mr Buckham came home that evening, Robert told him that the Watsons had drowned. When asked the reason, he was told 'suicide'.

The following morning, Superintendent Marden visited the scene. A doctor who examined the bodies put forward the theory that they had both been shot from behind. The boys were questioned and Robert soon broke down. He told Marden that his brother Richard had shot the Watsons; 'Go on Dick, tell them you did it.' Their home was searched and two guns found. The boys were arrested and both charged with murder and committed to the next Assize.

They appeared at the Essex Assize in November 1906. Robert was acquitted, but Richard's defence lawyers did not deny his culpability. It had been necessary to reload the gun to fire a third shot into Mrs Watson. Instead, they concentrated on his mental stability. He admitted to torturing and killing pets and animals, and complained of headaches. This medical defence was not sufficiently convincing. The jury were not convinced. There were three wounds so the gun had to have been deliberately reloaded. The brothers then entered the victim's home and a watch and some money was stolen. It may be that they were making a clumsy attempt to conceal the real nature of the crime. The jury returned a verdict of guilty and Richard was executed at Chelmsford Prison on 4 December by Henry Pierrepoint.

★

This has been a brief look at the career of one individual officer who served in the nineteenth and twentieth centuries, '...a most zealous and astute officer (with) untiring energies in the cause of law and justice'. However, Marden's successful career suddenly took a turn for the worse when, in 1912, he was suspended from duty, the subject of an enquiry into various offences, some dating back to 1903. These included illegally questioning prisoners, telling lies, using bad language and being disrespectful towards the Chief Constable and principal officers of the Standing Joint Committee. Marden appeared before a disciplinary hearing, was found guilty and reduced to the rank of inspector; his pay reduced to £110 per annum. The precise details of these allegations are unknown, although it is believed that some involved Dougal and the Moat Farm case.

This is not quite the end of the story. Despite retiring in 1913, Marden seems to have remained a policeman at heart, for in December 1920 he appeared before Grays Magistrates on a charge for impersonating a police officer. He was fined £5 and warned by the Standing Joint Committee that any further offences might mean the loss of his pension.

Fourteen

THE SILENT DETECTIVE

The names of Edwin and Robert Churchill will be unknown to most readers, but these two men, uncle and nephew, were to give expert evidence in the field of forensic ballistics in two of the most notorious murder cases to have occurred in Essex. The murders were separated by over a quarter of a century and in each, the evidence they gave was to lead to conviction and the gallows.

Edwin John Churchill was a gun maker who established a business in The Strand, London in the last quarter of the last century and was to become a gun expert consulted frequently by Scotland Yard. He was joined by his nephew Robert in the last two years of Queen Victoria's reign.

In those early days the evidence offered was limited to a report on the calibre and condition of the weapons and the calibre and weight of the bullets. Churchill carried out experiments, firing bullets into sheep's heads, which he conveniently obtained from the butcher's next door to his shop in The Strand. From these experiments he was able to determine from the comparison of powder marks, penetration and destruction of tissue whether the bullet wound in the victim was self-inflicted or otherwise.

But the science of ballistics was improving and in 1899, in France, a man was convicted of murder involving a firearm, by evidence linking marks made on the bullet with a gun in his possession.

In 1903, a body was discovered in a drainage ditch at Moat Farm, Clavering, Essex (see chapter 13). They were the remains of Camille Cecille Holland who had been murdered some four years before by Samuel Herbert Dougal, an unsavoury character, a womaniser, who had swept the 56-year-old wealthy spinster off her feet, only to murder her within three weeks and hide her body in the drainage ditch. He then set about forging her signature and until his arrest obtained large sums of money from her bank account.

Robert Churchill using his comparison microscope.

Dougal appeared before Mr Justice Wright, at the Essex Summer Assizes at Chelmsford in June 1903, charged with the wilful murder of Miss Holland. The circumstances of the case are well known and it is sufficient to focus on the involvement of Churchill in the case. The body, when discovered, was in a poor state and Miss Holland was only identified by the shoes she was wearing (currently on display in the Essex Police Museum). However, a post-mortem revealed she had been shot in the head.

Churchill examined ammunition found at the farm and conducted experiments with a sheep's head and was able to produce the same fracture in the lead as the bullet found in Miss Holland's skull. From this he was able to say that the bullet was fired from a revolver (recovered from Moat Farm), at a distance of six to twelve inches.

The trial lasted two days and Dougal was found guilty of the murder after the jury had deliberated for only ninety minutes. He was hanged at Chelmsford Prison on 14 July.

Robert Churchill was born in 1886 and at the time of the Dougal case was still learning his trade with his uncle. When Edwin died in 1910, Robert took over the family business, which at that time was in dire financial straits.

He was first called as an expert witness at a murder trial in 1910 at the age of 24, the first of many cases he was involved with during an illustrious career that was to last until his death in 1958.

Forensic ballistics may be simply defined as the relationship of the parts of a firearm with the bullets that come out of it. Major Calvin Goddard, the American expert, in an article in the journal of *Criminal Law and Criminology* in 1926 said:

> Every pistol barrel . . . contains minute irregularities which are peculiar to it alone, and which will never be reproduced in any other. These irregularities leave their marks . . . on every bullet fired from this barrel, and they constitute to all intents and purposes, a fingerprint of that particular barrel.

To aid investigation, the comparison microscope was used. It was a complex instrument which took several years to develop and evidence obtained by its use was first given in America in 1927.

Churchill toured America in that year and on his return had his own comparison microscope built. It was to become known as 'The Silent Detective'.

One of the earliest and perhaps most famous case Churchill was involved in occurred in Essex. In the early hours of 27 September 1927, the body of Constable George Gutteridge of the Essex Constabulary was found lying in the road at Stapleford Abbots. He had been shot four times in the head, including a bullet through each eye. A huge manhunt was started for the killer or killers but from the outset his murder was connected with the theft of a motor vehicle from Billericay on the same night, which was subsequently found abandoned in Stockwell, London.

The scene of PC Gutteridge's murder at Stapleford Abbotts.

WEBLEY REVOLVER
found fully loaded by
P.C. Bevis, Met Police
in Browne's car at
Clapham Junction,
21st January, 1928.

Above: The Webley revolver used by Browne to murder PC Gutteridge in 1927.

Right: Some of the ballistic evidence which helped to convict Brown and Kennedy of the murder.

The brutal killing of PC Gutteridge shocked the nation, and, within a few hours, Scotland Yard were called in. Chief Inspector James Berrett, an experienced detective, was put in charge of the case. At the scene two .45 bullets were prized out of the road surface and at the subsequent post-mortem on Gutteridge two more bullets were recovered.

Meanwhile, the stolen vehicle was found abandoned in Stockwell and a search revealed an empty cartridge case, marked RVIV on the floor. There was also blood on the runningboard of the car. The search for the persons responsible for the crime extended over the whole country and even abroad, but it was not until January 1928 that evidence came to light that implicated Frederick Guy Browne, a well known London criminal with a garage business in Clapham. The bullets and the cartridge case were handed to Churchill for examination. Although they were deformed the bullets retained sufficient rifling characteristics for Churchill to establish they had been fired from a Webley revolver.

The Metropolitan Police kept watch and Browne was arrested as he returned to his premises in Clapham. He was found in possession of a number of loaded firearms, including a .45 Webley revolver.

A further suspect was William Kennedy, an associate of Browne, who had fled London and returned to Liverpool, where he was well known to the Liverpool City Police. Observations were kept on an address and he was eventually arrested, but not before he

Above & below. The procession and funeral service for PC Gutteridge at Brentwood cemetery.

tried to shoot the police officer attempting to arrest him. It was only the fact that the gun jammed that saved the officer's life.

Kennedy was brought to London where he was interviewed by Berrett and admitted being present at the murder, but implicated Browne as the man who had killed Gutteridge. Browne was to deny any involvement in the murder right from the start, but a damning piece of evidence had been found.

Robert Churchill now examined the weapons recovered from Browne and was able to prove, by the use of the comparison microscope, that the empty cartridge case found in the stolen vehicle had been fired from the Webley revolver found in Browne's possession when he was arrested. The only defence that Browne could offer was that he had obtained the gun from Kennedy after the murder had occurred.

Both men appeared at the Central Criminal Court, before Mr Justice Avory, and evidence was heard from some forty prosecution witnesses, including four ballistics experts. It was through the use of photographs that Churchill proved to the court that the markings on the cartridge case matched those on the revolver.

Both men were convicted and suffered the ultimate penalty. Kennedy had admitted his part in the killing but Browne went to the gallows still protesting his innocence. Kennedy was executed at Wandsworth and Brown at Pentonville. PC Gutteridge left a wife and two small children. His widow received a pension of £78 4s 3d a year, and allowances of £15 12s 10d a year were also granted to the two children.

Note: The bullets and Webley revolver used to kill Gutteridge are in the Essex Police Museum, whilst other exhibits relating to Browne and Kennedy are in the Crime Museum at Scotland Yard.

Fifteen

'AND MAY THE LORD HAVE MERCY...'

The sentence of the Court upon you, is that you be taken from this place to a lawful prison and thence to a place of execution and that you be hanged by the neck until you are dead; and that your body be afterwards buried within the precincts of the prison in which you shall be confined before your execution. And may the Lord have mercy on your soul ... Amen.

The infamous words above were the basis of the death sentence passed on thousands of unfortunate criminals in British courts from the Middle Ages to 1965, when the death penalty in Britain was abolished for murder. In Essex, serious criminal cases were traditionally heard at the twice yearly Assizes in Chelmsford, (a third Assize would be held before Christmas if there were enough capital offence cases). For those receiving the ultimate punishment, execution traditionally took place at Moulsham Gaol, and from October 1825 the newly completed Springfield Prison, where forty-three individuals fell victim of the executioner's rope in the years up to the end of 1914.

The prison's main entrance was originally through an austere stone-built porter's lodge in the middle of the Springfield Road frontage. The lodge's flat roof was designed to support the gallows scaffold and drop, while the forecourt could easily accommodate the hundreds, and sometimes thousands, of spectators that would congregate for an execution.

The first execution

The first man to be hanged at Springfield Prison was James Winter, alias Reuben Martin, who was executed on 10 December 1827. He had been found guilty of the murder of Thomas Patrick, landlord of the Yorkshire Grey public house in Colchester. Patrick had

THE AWFUL FATE OF AN INCENDIARY.

Engraving showing the execution of 16-year-old James Cook, at the entrance to Springfield Gaol, for setting fire to his employers premises.

called the local constable to deal with the disorder that had arisen from an attempt by Winter to rob a man who had attended a sale held at the pub. Winter, angry at Patrick's interference, struck and killed him with a heavy board. Following the execution, Winter's body was left to hang for the prescribed hour, visible from the hips upward to the onlookers below. The corpse was cut down and given to the prison surgeon for dissection, all the while viewed by many prominent local men.

Eleven days later John Turner, alias Harris or Newman, was also dispatched to meet his maker. Turner was the head of a gang of thieves in the Runwell area who had been convicted of a robbery at Ramsden Crays. Two accomplices received sentences of 'Death recorded and reprieved.'

The following year, 1828, saw four executions at Springfield Prison. After the Summer Assize, John Williams was hanged for horse stealing at Epping. In December Michael Cashon and John Brien were executed for assault at East Ham, and Robert Oades hanged for the offence of horse stealing at Staines. Oades' body was taken by his mother and lay for a while at the nearby Three Cups Inn. He was buried in 'convenient, but unconsecrated ground' but his body was subsequently removed 'by persons unknown'.

The only execution in 1829 was that of 16-year-old James Cook, who was hanged on 27 March for setting on fire the premises of Witham farmer William Green, with whom he lived as a cow boy.

In 1830 there were four hangings, the most noteworthy being that of Captain William Moir on 2 August for the murder of William Malcolm, a fisherman, at Stanford-le-Hope in March 1830. Captain Moir had found Malcolm trespassing on his estate and, having previously warned Malcolm about the offence, Moir shot him to teach him a lesson. Afterwards the Captain took his injured victim to a surgeon for attention, but lockjaw set in and Malcolm died. Moir was executed despite pleas for clemency. His body was spared from dissection and returned to his family estate for burial.

Moir was followed to the gallows by John Stammers, convicted of 'an unnatural crime' at Walton. He was probably the first man interred in the triangular burial ground between the prison and Sandford Road, consecrated on 28 July 1830 by the Bishop of London. The other two hangings in 1830 were James Ewan, for arson at Rayleigh, and Thomas Bateman, for highway robbery and attempted murder at Lindsell.

Arson, rape and murder

The following year, 36-year-old William Jennings was executed for setting fire to a house at Writtle and in 1832, John Hills met the same fate for rape at Chelmsford. Jennings was the first local job for William Calcraft, who was born at Little Baddow in 1800, and who served as executioner from 1829 until 1874.

Two executions in 1835 were both for arson, George Cranfield for the offence at Bures and James Passfield at Mr Davie's farm at Toppesfield. These were the last occasions at Springfield when executions were for crimes other than murder or attempted murder. Davie had previously given evidence against Passfield when he was given a sixteen-month sentence for sheep stealing. By coincidence, Passfield was married to the widow of John Turner, the second man executed at Springfield, back in 1827. Some 1,200 spectators viewed the hanging on 27 March 1835, many of them farm labourers reputedly sent by their employers to witness what happened as a warning. The execution was delayed as the first rope was too short and another had to be substituted.

William Calcraft

'I hope I shall meet you in heaven'

Over the next sixteen years there were just two more executions. In March 1839, Abraham Hilliard was hanged for shooting Susanna Playle, an innkeeper, at Mountnessing after she had spurned his advances. Hilliard's last words were 'Goodbye, goodbye all; I hope I shall meet you in heaven'.

With the formation of the Essex Constabulary in 1840, police officers began to attend executions for public order purposes. Their first real test was on 14 August 1848, when 38-year-old Mary May was executed for the murder of her brother William Constable, alias Spratty Watts, at Wix. She was the first woman to be executed at the prison and the event attracted over 3,000 spectators.

'Clavering Church by Moonlight'. Painting by Chris Rowley. Sarah Chesham was buried in Clavering churchyard at night 'without benefit of clergy'. (© Chris Rowley)

Double execution draws crowds

On 25 March 1851, the double execution took place of Sarah Chesham and Thomas Drory. Drory's victim was the daughter-in-law of an old servant of his father, who was expecting his child. She was strangled in a field after she arranged to meet him at Doddinghurst to ask him to marry her. Forty-two-year-old Chesham had previously been acquitted of poisoning two of her own children and another child between 1845 and 1847. She met her end after being convicted for attempted murder by poisoning her husband, Richard, with arsenic at Clavering. Between 700 and 1,000 people watched the double execution.

Over the next twenty years there were a further five executions at Springfield; in 1853 Charles Saunders for murder at Chadwell, in 1857 Michael Crawley for wife murder at Stratford, and Charles Finch for murdering his sweetheart at Rivenhall, in 1864 Francis Wane for murder at Dagenham, and in 1865 Ferdinand Kohl for murder at Plaistow Marsh. Kohl's was to be the last public execution at the prison – the 1868 Capital Punishment Amendment Act ensured that all future hangings took place within the prison itself, away from morbid onlookers.

The first private execution

The first 'private' execution at Springfield was that of Michael Campbell on 24 April 1871. The 28-year-old Berwick-born tailor and former soldier was convicted of the murder of Samuel Galloway, a retired dock worker in Stratford, who was killed after giving chase to Campbell and three accomplices after they tried to break into his home at Cannon Street, Stratford. Mrs Galloway witnessed the assault and was able to identify Campbell as the assailant; when Galloway died ten days later, Campbell was charged with murder. He admitted his guilt but denied any intent.

Four years later, soldier Gunner Richard Coates of the Royal Artillery was executed on 29 March for the murder of a young girl, Alice Boughen, at Aveley. He had beaten her to death in a school closet after attempting to violate her. He was arrested after being spotted unsuccessfully attempting to carry her body to a river. He confessed his guilt in the condemned cell and blamed it on drink.

A gardener murders his wife

The next execution at the prison was Charles Revell, a gardener, on 29 July 1878 for the murder of his 23-year-old wife, Hester, in Epping Forest. Following lunch with her parents on 10 June, Revell went out to fetch some ale for them all to share. When he returned home over an hour later he was drunk. Revell and his wife began to quarrel over money when she grabbed him by the lapels and struck him. He knocked her to the ground and fled from the house. Against advice from her family she followed him into the forest where her body was discovered the next day, her throat cut from ear to ear.

Police Inspector shot dead

On 18 May 1885, James Lee was hanged for shooting dead Inspector Simmons of the Essex Constabulary who, with a colleague, had approached three men suspected of being about to commit a burglary at Rainham. Two of the men pulled out pistols and minutes later Simmons fell, mortally wounded. All three men fled but James Lee was later arrested and convicted at the Old Bailey. David Dredge was detained but was able to provide the unusual but successful alibi that he had not shot Inspector Simmons because at the time he was shooting at another police officer. The third suspect, James Martin, remained at large for nearly a year until he was involved in a robbery near Gretna and the murder of another policeman whilst trying to evade capture. He was hanged at Carlisle on 8 February 1886.

Lee was followed by 17-year-old Joseph Morley, executed on 21 November 1887 for the murder at Chigwell Row of a young married woman with whom he lodged by cutting her throat with a razor. After sentence was passed, he confessed that he had killed the woman, Mrs Rogers, but denied that when he entered her room he had intended to kill her.

On 15 August the next year George Sargent, a railway labourer and sometime poacher from Copford, was hanged for murdering his 21-year-old estranged wife Annie. They had been married for just a year when she left him, fed up with his drunken and violent behaviour, and returned to her mother's at Wakes Colne. When she refused Sargent's pleas to come home, he became enraged, grabbed her by her hair, locked her head between his knees and cut her throat from ear to ear with a clasp knife, almost severing her head. He ran away after the crime but was caught hiding in fields near the house.

Tobacco causes crime of passion

Thomas Sadler, a labourer, was hanged on 18 August 1891 for killing his lover's husband, William Wass, at Colchester by stabbing him with a penknife behind the ear during a dispute over custody of Sadler's children.

On 16 August 1893, John Davis was executed for battering Sergeant Adam Eves to death, whose body had been found in a ditch at Purleigh (see chapter 3). He was one of three poachers who were charged, two of whom were found to have bloodstains on their clothes, which they claimed were from an animal. The jury took less than half an hour to find 34-year-old Davis and his younger brother Richard guilty; the third man, Ramsey, not guilty. John Davis made a full confession while awaiting execution, which partially exonerated his brother, who was granted an eleventh-hour reprieve.

The following year, on 4 December, James Canham Read, a middle-aged married bookkeeper at the London Docks was executed for the murder of one of his several mistresses, 18-year-old Florence Dennis. She was found shot in a field at Prittlewell.

He had been arrested after police traced a telegram he had sent to a relative. (See chapter 13)

The next execution was again the result of a crime of passion. William Wilkes, a Canewdon shepherd, was hanged on 19 July 1898 for murdering his wife by kicking her to death after they had quarrelled over some tobacco. As the executioner placed the noose around his neck, Wilkes turned to the warder in tears and asked whether it would hurt him. Before the warder could reply he was dropped 7ft 2in to his death.

The final execution of the century at Springfield was that of Samuel Crozier, the landlord of the Admiral Rous Inn at Galleywood Common, who was hanged on 5 December 1899. On 25 June he assaulted his wife, Ann, in a room above the pub. She died from her injuries the next day but the doctor, unaware of the fight, stated that the death was from natural causes as a result of a fall. Word soon reached the police about the fight and, less than an hour after his wife's funeral, Crozier was in custody. He was initially charged with manslaughter and later with murder.

The Moat Farm murder

On 3 October 1900, William Burrett became the executioner's first victim of the twentieth century. The 35-year-old unemployed hawker had been convicted of fatally stabbing his prostitute wife, Ada, after she had told him that she did not intend to support him from her earnings. The trial, which took place at the Old Bailey, only lasted two days, such was the overwhelming evidence against Burrett.

The perpetrator of the famous Moat Farm murder was the next visitor to the gallows at Springfield. He was a 57-year-old former Sergeant Major of the Royal Engineers, Samuel Herbert Dougal, who was executed on 14 July 1903. (See chapter 13.)

His execution caused a controversy when it was alleged that a confession on the scaffold was badgered from him by an overzealous chaplain.

Less than three months later, on 1 December 1903, another soldier, 21-year-old Bernard White of the Essex Regiment, was executed for beating to death his 20-year-old ex-girlfriend, Maud Garret, at Warley Gap, having discovered that she was seeing someone else. This was the first Springfield execution at which the famous hangman Henry Pierrepoint had officiated.

Christmas quarrels and cut-throats

Pierrepoint was in action a year later when 20-year-old Richard Buckham was hanged on 4 December 1904 for shooting dead an elderly married couple named Watson during a robbery at their bungalow in Basildon. Buckham's brother was also charged, but acquitted. (See chapter 13.)

Pierrepoint's last execution was that of 45-year-old farm labourer Frederick Foreman on 14 July 1910. Foreman had battered to death the woman he lived with, Elizabeth Eley, at East Farm, Wennington after the couple argued on their way home from a Whit Monday drinking session.

Another quarrel, on Christmas Eve the same year, at Stratford between 19-year-old gas worker George Newton and his fiancée, Ada Roker, resulted in murder when Newton cut the 21-year-old's throat. He was executed at Springfield Prison on 31 January 1911 after his plea of insanity failed.

Coincidentally, a very similar murder occurred late the following year and led to the execution of 20-year-old William Beal on 10 December 1912. He too had murdered his fiancée, 17-year-old Clara Carter, again in Stratford, and again by cutting her throat as they kissed under a street lamp, after her parents forbade the couple from seeing one another. Beal also cut his own throat, and when he was hanged a large gash opened in his neck.

The oldest man to be hanged this century in Britain was 71-year-old German-born grocer Charles Fremd, who was executed on 4 November 1914 for murdering his wife at Leytonstone. She was found dead from a cut throat. Her husband was beside her with only a minor self-inflicted wound. As Fremd was dropped, he caught and bruised his head on the trapdoor. Shortly after Fremd's death the prison was taken over by the army for use as a military gaol, and after it reverted to civilian use in 1931 there were no further executions. Thus, the oldest man was also the last man to feel the noose around his neck at Springfield Prison.

ABOUT THE AUTHOR

Martyn Lockwood worked for the Essex Police for forty-three years (retiring in 2011), thirty of them as a serving police officer. He is currently secretary to the Trustees of the Essex Police Museum and also the Essex Police Memorial Trust.

He has written a number of articles on policing and crime in Essex, and his first book – *The Essex Police Force: A History* – was published in 2009.

Other titles published by The History Press

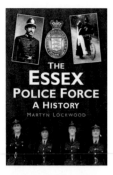

The Essex Police Force: A History

MARTYN LOCKWOOD

This book tells the history of the Essex Police Force; from its inception in 1840, through to the present day. Illustrated with over 180 photographs and documents, it features images of policemen and women at work and at leisure, together with changing modes of transport, scene of crime photographs and mugshots of Victorian criminals. This volume provides a glimpse into some of the events and people that have shaped the force we know today.

978 0 7524 5167 1

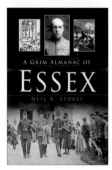

A Grim Almanac of Essex

NEIL R. STOREY

Neil R. Storey's macabre calendar chronicles the shadier side of life in Essex. Murderers and footpads, pimps and prostitutes, riots, rebels, bizarre funerals, disaster and peculiar medicine all feature. The book is richly illustrated with engravings, newspaper reports, photographs and original documents. It is horrible, if it is ghastly, if it is strange, then it is here! If you have the stomach for it, then read on.

978 0 7524 6510 4

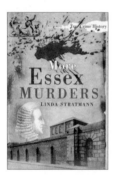

More Essex Murders

LINDA STRATMANN

This chilling follow-up to *Essex Murders* brings together more true cases, dating between 1823 and 1960, that shocked not only the county but also made headline news across the nation. They include the bloody killing of a police sergeant, a murder carried out in the depths of Epping Forest, the Dutch au pair found dead in a ditch, and a case that made criminal history in which the accused said he had strangled the victim while he was asleep.

978 0 7524 5850 2

Paranormal Essex

JASON DAY

Visit the 'Most Haunted House in England' in Borley, encounter the Spider of Stock, witness an RAF pilot's shocking near miss with a UFO over the skies of Southend, and find out how the infamous 'Witchfinder General' served as judge, jury and executioner in Manningtree. With accounts of hauntings, ley lines, UFOs and Big Cats, this extensive collection of paranormal reports includes previously unpublished accounts from the author's personal case files.

978 0 7524 5527 3

Visit our website and discover thousands of other History Press books.

www.thehistorypress.co.uk

The History Press